AARON RODGERS
LEADER OF THE PACK

ROB REISCHEL

For Laura, Maddie, and Mia—the best team in town

This book is available in quantity at special discounts for your group or organization.
For further information contact:

Triumph Books
542 South Dearborn Street
Suite 750
Chicago, IL 60605
Phone: (312) 939-3330
Fax: (312) 663-3557
www.triumphbooks.com

Printed in the United States of America
ISBN: 978-1-60078-645-7

Content packaged by Mojo Media, Inc.
Joe Funk: Editor
Jason Hinman: Creative Director

Photos on pages 19, 20, 21, 23, 24, 25, 27, 28, 29, and 53
© 2011 by Chico Enterprise-Record, reprinted with permission.

Photos on pages 1, 3, 48, 51, 166, and 174
© 2011 by Jim Biever, reprinted with permission.

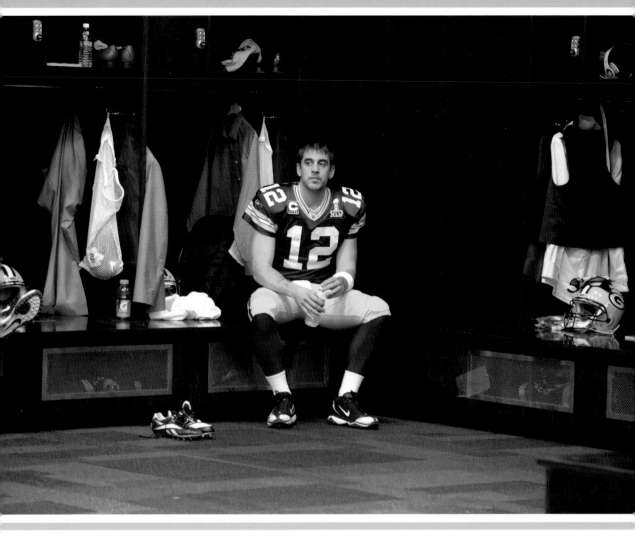

CONTENTS

PREFACE

Many of my colleagues in Wisconsin have covered the Green Bay Packers far longer than I have. And perhaps they've seen players come farther than Aaron Rodgers has.

But in my 10 years covering the Packers, Rodgers has improved more than anyone I've witnessed.

When Rodgers arrived in the spring of 2005, he was lost. Inaccurate. Overwhelmed. Frustrated.

But one thing Rodgers never lacked was confidence.

No matter how bad he looked—and there were times it wasn't pretty—he never doubted himself. Today, we know why.

Rodgers is smiling last, and smiling the widest, after leading the 2010 Green Bay Packers to a Super Bowl championship and winning Most Valuable Player honors.

With a postseason for the ages, Rodgers became one of just 29 quarterbacks to ever win Super Bowl titles. Rodgers joined Bart Starr and Brett Favre as the only Packers' signal-callers to win Super Bowls. And he's thrust himself into a discussion of the NFL's elite quarterbacks.

It's a remarkable transformation for a player that struggled immensely that first summer in Green Bay. Back then, Rodgers' delivery was mechanical. He didn't appear to have the athleticism he now possesses. And his arm strength, a major positive today, appeared only so-so back then.

Anyone that tells you they would have bet on Rodgers becoming a star is probably fibbing. There were no signs of it that first summer.

But Rodgers is as sharp as they come. He's bright, witty, and articulate. In fact, there are many days Rodgers will challenge the media as much as they challenge him.

So it was simply a matter of time before he grasped things mentally. What came as a surprise is how much he improved the other aspects of his game.

By Rodgers' second summer in Green Bay, he was a different player. By his third, he looked like starting material.

In fact, after Green Bay lost the 2007 NFC Championship Game to the New York Giants, one Packers assistant coach told me that many on the staff believed they would have defeated the Giants if Rodgers—not Favre—had been the quarterback that night.

Emboldened by that belief in Rodgers, it was easier for Green Bay to let Favre retire, then eventually trade him in the summer of 2008. Still, that lengthy soap opera made Rodgers a nationwide talking point.

While Rodgers' development as a player was significant by that time, his growth as a person came out here.

Each day, Rodgers was bombarded by questions about Favre, as well as his own future. What did Rodgers think about Favre wanting to return? Could he live with being a backup again? Did he still want to be in Green Bay? The questions were endless.

Rodgers was 24 years old at that time, and many people that age would have expressed frustration. Rodgers stayed the course and bit his tongue. He came off as professional and classy. He may have won more points for his behavior in that ordeal than any touchdown pass he's ever thrown.

Twelve months after the Favre saga, Rodgers and I sat together inside Lambeau Field shortly before training camp opened. We discussed football, life, and Favre.

"I think I earned a lot of fans nationally, who maybe didn't know me or know a lot about me, by handling things the way I did," Rodgers said. "It was a difficult situation, but I just tried to be as honest and as classy as I possibly could. I realized the situation was way bigger than myself, and I think in doing that, I earned the respect of my teammates, the organization, and our fans. And I think people that didn't know me nationally took notice, too."

They haven't stopped.

The Packers went just 6–10 that first year under Rodgers, but have risen since. First, there was a playoff appearance in 2009. Then, with expectations sky high in 2010, the Packers survived a glut of injuries and became Super Bowl champions.

Rodgers was the biggest reason why.

Rodgers' ascension to Super Bowl MVP is one of the NFL's most compelling stories. Remember, Rodgers had zero NCAA Division I scholarship offers coming out of high school, he plummeted down draft boards in April 2005, and he was forced to wait three years for his chance in Green Bay.

At every turn, Rodgers has faced long odds. Each time, he's succeeded.

"The guy has overcome a ton," teammate Jordy Nelson said. "A ton."

The next challenge will be for Rodgers to keep improving and help the Packers win multiple Super Bowls in the years ahead.

Back in the summer of 2005, I wouldn't have thought it possible that Rodgers would one day lead Green Bay to a Super Bowl. I was dead wrong.

You'll never catch me betting against him again.

—Rob Reischel

CHAPTER 1

A DREAM COME TRUE

Aaron Rodgers ducked under center Scott Wells, took the final snap of the 2010 season, and touched his left knee to the ground. Rodgers put the ball in his left hand, took off his helmet, and was then embraced by teammates from every angle. As confetti fell from Cowboys Stadium like snow on a Wisconsin winter day, Rodgers made his way to a football-shaped podium in the center of the field. There, America's newest "Golden Boy" hoisted the Vince Lombardi Trophy and was given his signature title belt by teammate Clay Matthews.

The Green Bay Packers were NFL champions once again, courtesy of their thrilling 31–25 win over Pittsburgh in the Super Bowl XLV. And Rodgers—who was named the game's Most Valuable Player—was the biggest reason why Green Bay could be called Titletown once again. "It is

a dream come true," Rodgers said that night. "It's what I dreamt about as a little kid watching Joe Montana and Steve Young, and we just won the Super Bowl."

Rodgers had just finished a Super Bowl performance—and a playoff run—that rivaled any the NFL has ever seen. He carved up a Pittsburgh defense that was allowing an NFL-best 14.5 points per game by throwing three touchdown passes and completing 24-of-39 passes for 304 yards. He then joined Bart Starr as the only quarterbacks in Packers history to be named MVP of a Super Bowl. That capped a memorable postseason in which Rodgers threw for 1,094 yards and nine touchdown passes. The only quarterback prior to Rodgers to throw for more than 1,000 yards and nine TDs in one postseason was Kurt Warner.

Rodgers had led the Packers to three

Aaron Rodgers is all smiles during player introductions before a 2010 preseason scrimmage. And why not—the Packers were being picked by many as the favorite to win it all.

"IT'S WHAT I DREAMT ABOUT AS A LITTLE KID WATCHING JOE MONTANA AND STEVE YOUNG

—Aaron Rodgers

road wins and helped Green Bay become the first No. 6 seed from the NFC to ever reach a Super Bowl. Then, Packers head coach Mike McCarthy put the entire offense on Rodgers' shoulders in the title game, and he was the No. 1 reason Green Bay defeated the vaunted Steelers. Thanks to one magical postseason run, the names Brady, Manning, and Brees aren't alone today when discussing the NFL's top quarterback. Rodgers is now part of the discussion.

"I think it tells the world that Aaron is real," Wells said afterward. "There were a lot of questions this postseason coming from the exterior, outside of our own locker room. We always had confidence in him and what he's been able to do. He's our guy, we love him, and I think this man has silenced some of the doubters out there."

Rodgers has faced doubters every step of his remarkable journey. And it could be argued that of the 29 quarterbacks to now win Super Bowls, Rodgers overcame the most obstacles and longest odds to reach football's pinnacle. Undersized in high school, Rodgers didn't receive a single NCAA Division I scholarship offer. He went the junior college route, before University of California coach Jeff Tedford discovered him.

Rodgers waited, waited, and waited some more during the 2005 NFL Draft before the Packers finally took him with the 24th overall pick. Then Rodgers played the waiting game for three years while he sat behind Packers icon Brett Favre. "He has had a hard road for no reason," Packers wideout Jordy Nelson said. "He was behind Brett. Give him credit for learning and not just sitting there and waiting for Brett to be done. He went about and perfected his game. He stepped up, and you see where we are now."

It's unlikely the Packers would have

Green Bay quarterback Aaron Rodgers, shown scrambling from danger during Super Bowl XLV, had the entire offense placed on his shoulders that night—and delivered.

been in this position had they caved in to the indecisive Favre during the summer of 2008. Favre had retired that March, then changed his mind and wanted to return. But the Packers believed they had something special with Rodgers and made the controversial move of trading Favre, a sure-fire, first-ballot Hall of Famer. Three years later, Rodgers made general manager Ted Thompson and head coach Mike McCarthy look like geniuses when he vanquished the ghost of Favre.

"I've never felt like there's been a monkey on my back," Rodgers said. "The organization stood behind me, believed in me. I told Ted back in 2005 he wouldn't be sorry with this pick. I told him in '08 that I was going to repay their trust and get us this opportunity." As unlikely as Rodgers' story is, the tale of the 2010 Green Bay Packers is equally improbable.

Ravaged by injuries unlike any Green Bay team in more than three decades, the 2010 Packers were a constant work in progress. By the time the regular season ended, 15 players had gone to the injured reserve list, and eight of those started at least one game. "We've had some adversity," Matthews said. "We've had to fight

Pittsburgh's defense came into Super Bowl XLV ranked first in the NFL in points allowed (14.5), but Aaron Rodgers and the Packers erupted for 31 points against the vaunted Steelers.

through it all season. We had some key contributors go down. The young guys stepped up. The playmakers on this team continued to take their game to a whole other level."

There were plenty of potholes, though. Green Bay lost consecutive overtime games in mid-October and found itself a disappointing 3–3. But a four-game winning streak—highlighted by a pair of victories over Favre and the Minnesota Vikings—got the season steered back in the right direction.

Just when it appeared Green Bay had battled through its injury woes, Rodgers suffered a concussion in the second quarter of a Week 14 game in Detroit. Rodgers missed the rest of that game and the following week in New England. The Packers lost both of those contests and were just 8–6 with two games remaining. "Those last couple of games of the regular season—we had to win those games," cornerback Charles Woodson said. "It felt like a playoff game for us."

And Green Bay played that way, too. Rodgers had arguably the finest performance of his career during a 45–17 destruction of the visiting New York Giants. Then in the regular season finale, Rodgers and the Packers rallied past a Chicago team trying to knock Green Bay out of the postseason. The Packers were into the tournament, but they had to do something no NFC team had ever accomplished: reach the Super Bowl as a No. 6 seed.

"We always believe. We know who we are," said linebacker Desmond Bishop, Rodgers' teammate at Cal. "We know the talent we have on this team. And, we just had to figure out a way to put it all together. When we won our last two games, it all clicked. Relentless pursuit of perfection and we found greatness." They sure did, and so did their 27-year-old quarterback.

A quarterback's reputation is built by what he does in the playoffs, and that's why today, Rodgers' stock has never been higher. First, he led the Packers to three straight road wins, then they knocked off a Pittsburgh team that had won two of the last four Super Bowls. Suddenly, talk of Rodgers not being able to win a big game seemed laughable.

"One thing, that guy is a true leader," wideout Donald Driver said. "He goes out

Pittsburgh linebacker James Harrison is one of football's fiercest players. Despite relentless pressure, Aaron Rodgers stood in against Harrison and the Steelers' pass rush and led the Packers to victory.

week in and week out and proves people wrong. He proved it once again, and he can now say that he is one of the best quarterbacks in this game." There would be few arguments after what Rodgers did in the 2010 postseason.

First, he carved up a Philadelphia defense by throwing three TDs and outplaying Michael Vick during a Wild Card win over the Eagles. It was Green Bay's first playoff win ever in Philadelphia. Then it was on to Atlanta where Rodgers had a performance for the ages. Three TD passes. A ridiculous passer rating of 136.8. A completion percentage of 86.1 percent. And zero Packers punts. Green Bay trampled the NFC's top seed, 48–21, and Rodgers was becoming one of football's hottest names. "He was on fire," Packers coach Mike McCarthy said of Rodgers. "He likes playing in domes, and you can see why."

Rodgers and Green Bay's offense weren't as sharp during a 21–14 win over Chicago in the NFC Championship Game. But the Packers were good enough to beat their oldest rival in the 182nd—and most important—meeting in this remarkable series.

For the first time in 13 years, Green Bay had won the NFC and would play for an NFL championship. "It's an unbelievable feeling," said rookie cornerback Sam Shields, who had two interceptions against the Bears, including one in the closing moments. "There's a lot of guys that waited a long, long time for this."

Rodgers' wait to reach football's grandest stage wasn't necessarily lengthy, but it was filled with far more questions than most Super Bowl quarterbacks are ever presented. Would a scholarship offer ever come around? Why did 21 teams—including Dallas and Minnesota twice—pass on Rodgers during the 2005 NFL Draft? Would Favre ever leave? And finally, could Rodgers adequately replace one of the greatest quarterbacks in NFL history and win over a fan base?

"I think he's a very mature young man," Thompson said of Rodgers. "In some ways sitting for three years and then playing is helpful. That's the way it was back in the day. You always brought quarterbacks in, and you developed them for about two or three years before you actually played them—that's hard to do anymore. "I think

Packers quarterback Aaron Rodgers celebrates after throwing a first-half touchdown in Super Bowl XLV. Rodgers threw three touchdowns and no interceptions in the game.

that was helpful. He was able to sit back, watch, listen, and learn. Like I said, he's a very good quarterback, and I think the best is yet to come."

Thompson was right. The best came in the 45th Super Bowl, where Rodgers had the weight of the offense on his shoulders and delivered with an unforgettable night. "He is the reason they won," Steelers defensive lineman Brett Kiesel said. Indeed. Never forget, this was football's best defense Rodgers was dissecting. The Steelers simply don't allow teams to run the ball. And if you become one-dimensional, Pittsburgh pass rushers like James Harrison and LaMarr Woodley start licking their chops.

Rodgers never blinked, though. He made quick decisions, was remarkably accurate, and showed courage against the rush as Green Bay threw the ball on 39 of its 52 offensive plays (75 percent). "He played a great game," Packers left tackle Chad Clifton said. "He made a lot of plays out there today from inside the pocket and outside the pocket. He is a phenomenal quarterback."

Afterward, the Packers were NFL champions for a league-high 13th time. And Rodgers was not only a Super Bowl champion, but an MVP as well. Every question had been answered. His wait was officially over. "It's a special honor to be one of the leaders of this football team," Rodgers said. "I've said it once, and I'll say it again: no one person has ever won a game by themselves. This is a team effort and a great group of men. Special guys, and I'm just blessed to be one of the leaders on this team.

"Individually, it's the top of the mountain in my sport, my profession. It's what you dream about as a kid and think about in high school, junior college, D-I: getting this opportunity and what would you do? I'm fortunate and blessed to play for a team that believes in us. At the same time, I wanted to make sure I was the most prepared guy on the field to have this type of performance."

Rodgers most certainly was. In many ways, though, he had been preparing his whole life. ∎

Green Bay Packers quarterback Aaron Rodgers was named the Most Valuable Player of Super Bowl XLV. Rodgers joined Bart Starr and Desmond Howard as the only Packers to earn that honor.

CHAPTER 2

THE PRIDE OF CHICO, CALIFORNIA

Football was always king to Aaron Rodgers. From his days at Whitford Middle School in Beaverton, Oregon, through a terrific career at Pleasant Valley High School in Chico, California, Rodgers always dreamed about playing in the NFL. He lived and died with the home state San Francisco 49ers. He even wore a Joe Montana T-shirt under his uniform as he got older.

Just one problem: when Rodgers entered high school, he was a scrawny 5-foot-2, 130 pounds. "He was little," said Ron Souza, Rodgers' quarterbacks coach at Pleasant Valley. "But he was very gifted for a little guy. He had excellent mechanics and always had a great understanding of football. Watching film, his readiness to learn, the whole mental part he was terrific at. And then he started growing."

Rodgers, the middle of three boys, was a late bloomer. By the time his senior season rolled around, though, he was 6-feet and 170 pounds. Rodgers lit it up his last two years at Pleasant Valley, throwing for more than 4,400 total yards during his junior and senior seasons combined. He also set school records for touchdown passes in a game (six), all-purpose yards (440), and twice was an all-section choice.

But Rodgers was far from a household name. And Chico, located 90 miles north of Sacramento, is hidden away in the Northern Sacramento Valley. So when Rodgers' high school season ended, not a single Division I school offered him a scholarship. "We just don't get a lot of exposure up there because maybe a lot of the coaches and players don't understand how to get the most exposure for your players,"

Aaron Rodgers was undersized at Pleasant Valley High School and didn't receive a single NCAA Division I scholarship offer.

Chico Enterprise-Record/Glenn Fuentes

Chico Enterprise-Record/Bill Husa

Rodgers said. "For me, I didn't go to any Nike camps, didn't get my name out there.

"We're north of Sacramento, and we just don't produce a lot of top athletes. You look at my high school team, and we had three guys who went on to play football ... so it's not like we've got a hot-bed of Division I athletes over there. So a lot of times when one does come along they get overlooked."

Craig Rigsbee, the head coach at nearby Butte College back then and its athletics director today, knew of Rodgers. Rigsbee had watched Rodgers in a passing league the previous summer and liked what he saw. Butte, a junior college of 5,600 full-time students, was located just

(above) Aaron Rodgers has a laugh with his parents, Ed and Darla Rogers. (opposite) Rodgers was clocked in the low 90s while pitching for Pleasant Valley High School in 2002.

15 miles outside of Chico. Rigsbee had turned the Roadrunners into a national power and thought Rodgers could be his next great quarterback.

Just one problem: Darla Rodgers. "I lived one cul-de-sac away from his family, so in January (of Rodgers' senior year) I walked over there one night," Rigsbee said. "Right away his mom, Darla, said, 'No kid of mine is going to a J.C.'" You can see why Darla Rodgers felt that way. Aaron Rodgers had a 3.5 grade point average and posted a 1,310 on his SATs, so his grades and test scores were good enough to qualify at many high-level academic institutions.

But as Rigsbee continued talking, the Rodgers family became believers. "Aaron was pretty down and not sure what he wanted to do next," Rigsbee said. "But I started explaining about our academic process and how you have to take general courses your freshman year and how all the credits transfer. Then I explained how much success we've had at Butte and how I could help put Aaron on a national stage." By the time Rigsbee left that night,

Rodgers was convinced. He had just one question. "He just said, 'Will you give me a fair shot to be the quarterback?'" Rigsbee recalled. "And I said I would."

Rigsbee was later put to the test on that promise. Butte had a returning quarterback named Brian Botts who was in his third year with the program. Botts had paid his dues, and most figured he would play in front of Rodgers. Rigsbee was extremely impressed with both players during practices that summer. But Rigsbee kept coming back to one play, more than any other. "By the time [Aaron] got to us, he had grown another inch and was maybe 195," Rigsbee said. "And on about the second day of practice, he threw a 50-yard dart back to the left. I turned to my assistants and said, 'Did you guys just see that?'"

Still, not everyone was convinced. At the end of camp, Rigsbee solicited the opinions of his assistant coaches on what to do at quarterback. "Every guy on the staff said they'd go with [Botts]," Rigsbee said. "Finally I said, 'This is why I'm the head coach. We're going with Aaron.' The kid had been here two weeks, and he was

After high school, Rodgers spent a year at Butte College in Chico, California.

Chico Enterprise-Record/Glenn Fuentes

already better than the kid that was here three years. And I said after a game or two, he's going to be 100 times better."

Botts left the program after two games. Rodgers led the Roadrunners to a 10–1 record, a No. 2 national ranking, and a Nor-Cal Conference championship. Rodgers threw for more than 2,400 yards, 28 TDs, and just four interceptions. Perhaps most importantly, though, Rodgers learned how to lead.

"That was the most important year of my young football career," Rodgers said Super Bowl week. "I learned a lot about myself that year, being an 18-year-old playing with guys from all over the country and different countries: Canadians, a

Rodgers faced an uphill battle to become the starting quarterback at Butte College. But once he did, he led the Roadrunners to a 10–1 record and a No. 2 national ranking.

Chico Enterprise-Record

25-year-old center, guys who had been to prison, guys who had been bounce-backs from Division I, local guys, and trying to be an 18-year-old and lead those guys and figure out a way to lead them. I learned a lot about leadership and a lot about myself, and I also got my confidence back because I had a real good season, so that was an important year. I still keep in touch with a lot of those guys and my coach as well."

Rigsbee had also promised Rodgers he would do everything possible to help him land a Division I scholarship after one season. So that October, Rigsbee arranged for University of California coach Jeff Tedford to attend practice. It's been widely reported that Tedford came that day to see Butte tight end Garrett Cross, who eventually went to Cal. That wasn't the case, though. "He was there to see Aaron," Rigsbee said. "And it was kind of a wild practice. We were throwing on every play and running 7-on-7 drills. I mean, we never ran 7-on-7s on Mondays, so guys were wondering what was going on. At the end of practice, Tedford came over to me and said, 'He's the best junior college quarterback I've ever seen.' And I just said, 'Right on!'"

Right on indeed, as Tedford offered Rodgers a scholarship that day. "Seeing him in person, he was very impressive," Tedford said. "He was very accurate, threw the ball well, and had a tight spiral. It was a very pleasant surprise to find out he was very strong in other categories as well."

Rodgers immediately showed that at Cal, too. He didn't win the starting job in fall camp that year, but he had claimed the position by Week 5. Rodgers led the Golden Bears to a 7–3 mark in their final 10 games and threw for 2,903 yards and 19 TDs. Rodgers, who's extremely protective of the ball, had streaks of 98 and 105 consecutive passes without an interception. He led the Bears to late-season wins against Washington and Stanford to clinch a berth in the Insight Bowl. Then Rodgers threw for 394 yards and was named MVP in Cal's bowl win over Virginia Tech.

Rodgers was even better the following year, when he guided the second-highest scoring offense in school history. Personally, Rodgers threw for 2,566 yards and 24 TDs, with just eight interceptions, and

Rodgers was discovered by University of California coach Jeff Tedford, who told Butte College coach Craig Rigsbee, "He's the best junior college quarterback I've ever seen."

Chico Enterprise-Record/Bill Husa

Chico Enterprise-Record

was named first-team all–Pacific 10.

After Rodgers' junior season, NFL scouts gave him a first-round grade, and many believed he would be taken extremely early in the draft. So he declared for the NFL Draft with one year of eligibility left. It was quite a journey for a player who couldn't get a glance from college recruiters just three years earlier. "Recruiters put so much into height and weight," Rodgers said. "I was a little under what I am now, and my area doesn't get heavily recruited, either. I'll tell you what: I'm a firm believer that everything happens for a reason."

In the weeks ahead, that philosophy would most certainly be put to the test. ■

In two years at California, Rodgers threw for more than 5,400 yards and 43 touchdowns.

CHAPTER 3

COMBINE HIGHS, DRAFT-DAY LOWS

Aaron Rodgers was one of the stars of the 2005 NFL Combine. Bright, articulate, personable, Rodgers was a hit almost everywhere he went. One night, Rodgers sat down with members of the Green Bay Packers front office. But with the Packers slated to pick at No. 24 in two months, both sides figured they wouldn't see each other again. "I remember telling them 'Trade up. I'd love to play for you guys,'" Rodgers recalled. "And they were saying, 'Well, you probably won't be available when we want to get you.'"

It was easy to think that way. Rodgers had enjoyed remarkable success at the University of California. In two seasons as a starter, Rodgers threw 43 touchdowns, 13 interceptions, and for nearly 5,500 yards. Rodgers had shown outstanding accuracy, evidenced by his 23 straight completions against USC, which tied an NCAA record. He also scored an impressive 35 on the 50-question Wonderlic test.

"I think I'm a student of the game," Rodgers said that February. "I think I pick up an offense pretty quickly. Prepare for a game, just watch a lot of film, know your opponent as well as knowing your own team and your strength. For me, it was tough this year because we lost a lot of receivers, so I had to continually work in practice to get the timing down with those guys. Just constant film study and the mental preparation, I think. Visualizing good plays in your mind so when it comes game time you've already seen yourself do that in your mind already, and it just becomes second nature, muscle memory."

On the flip side, the 6-foot-2 Rodgers was at least an inch shorter than many

Aaron Rodgers, shown here running the 40-yard dash at the 2005 NFL Combine, was projected to be one of the top picks in that year's draft.

teams wanted at the position. Although he weighed 223 pounds, it was clear he still needed to add bulk. But the biggest question Rodgers answered that week was about his delivery and playing for Cal coach Jeff Tedford.

Tedford turned the likes of David Carr, Kyle Boller, Trent Dilfer, Akili Smith, and Joey Harrington into college standouts and first-round NFL draft picks. But none matched that success at the next level. Green Bay general manager Ted Thompson remembers asking Rodgers about that very topic during their 15-minute get-together at the Combine. "We

(above) Fans Steve Tate, left, and Dan Kursevski look over possible picks during a Lambeau Field Atrium draft party on April 23, 2005. (right) Aaron Rodgers, joined by fellow draft prospects Cedric Benson, left, and Antrel Rolle, center, attempts to throw a ball through a tire during a New York television appearance prior to the 2005 NFL Draft.

"I KIND OF LIKE HIM TO HAVE A LITTLE BIT OF A CHIP ON HIS SHOULDER AND WANT TO PROVE THOSE CRITICS WRONG. —Darrell Bevell"

actually asked Aaron in our interview at Indy about that," Thompson said. "He says he's better than all of those guys, so we feel pretty good about that."

Darrell Bevell, who was Green Bay's quarterbacks coach at the time, remembered the exchange, as well. "It's kind of a tense atmosphere in that room," Bevell said. "You've got a young man (Rodgers) sitting there, you've got ... some pretty heavy hitters talking to him. You're really trying to get the questions that you want to get through, so you're kind of just taking it in. But I was impressed with him a little bit. I kind of like him to have a little bit of a chip on his shoulder and want to prove those critics wrong."

Rodgers seemed to win people over with his intelligence, confidence, and quick wit. And when Rodgers left Indianapolis that February, many expected San Francisco to make either him or University of Utah quarterback Alex Smith the No. 1 pick. The debate intensified even more after both had sublime workouts on their pro day.

Smith received a standing ovation after his performance. Rodgers didn't get quite as much love, but he certainly impressed. "Alex is a great player," Rodgers said. "It's funny because my first big game was his first big game. His first start was my first extended playing period at Cal, so I kind of followed his career from then. He's a little taller than I am, I think. We both put up some good numbers this year. I'm just excited about going up against him, being able to run against him, throw against him, and see how we stack up."

That decision eventually would be made by San Francisco head coach Mike Nolan, who was given total autonomy with

Rodgers acknowledges cheers from the audience after the Packers made him their first selection in the 2005 NFL Draft.

the No. 1 pick. And Rodgers was hopeful he'd made a lasting impression on Nolan—and the rest of the NFL brass at the Combine. "As time has gone on the last month or so, to me, I'm very confident there's going to be a guy who fits," Nolan said.

Indeed there was. Rodgers just didn't like who it was.

....

April 23, 2005, was supposed to be the best day of Aaron Rodgers' young life.

Rodgers was holding out hope that his home-state team—the San Francisco 49ers—would use the No. 1 pick in the NFL Draft on him. Even if that didn't happen, Rodgers figured to go early that day. Instead, Rodgers' stay inside the "Green Room" at the Jacob K. Javits Convention Center in New York City was almost hard to watch. "Well, obviously when you're sitting in the green room, you just want to get out of there," Rodgers said.

It took until the 24th pick that excruciating day before Rodgers heard his name called. That's when the Green Bay Packers threw Rodgers a net and broke his fall. "Did we think he was going to be there when we

Aaron Rodgers plummeted to the 24th overall pick in the 2005 NFL Draft before the Green Bay Packers broke his fall.

were watching tape? No," Thompson said. "But over the course of the last week or so there was a couple of, I don't know, websites, or ESPN, or something that said maybe he might get there. So, I went back and did a little more work just to make sure. But I feel very comfortable that this kid warranted being picked where we were at."

Just a few weeks earlier, it seemed incomprehensible that Rodgers would be around at pick No. 24. At one point, the 49ers were negotiating with representatives for Alex Smith, Braylon Edwards, and Rodgers about becoming the draft's top pick. When the 49ers decided on Smith, though, it sent Rodgers into a free fall. Only Cleveland, Tennessee, and Arizona were teams with top 10 picks that had a possible need at quarterback, and when they went in different directions, Rodgers kept spiraling. There were a couple more chances for Rodgers to find a landing spot inside the top 15. That didn't happen, though, and when Houston passed at No. 16, a string of teams with proven quarterbacks also went in different directions.

Green Bay was another team that ap- peared set at quarterback. But with Favre aging and always unsure about his future plans, Thompson selected the highest remaining player on his board. "When it got past 16 (Houston), we knew the teams at 17–23 probably weren't going to take me, and Green Bay was probably our next option," Rodgers said on draft day. "And the more I thought about it the more I realized it could be a great fit for me, being able to learn from one of the best quarterbacks of all time and to not be thrown in the fire right away and to come to a team with a storied franchise and a winning tradition. I think it's going to be exciting. It's going to be a great fit."

In Thompson's mind, he had gotten a steal. The Packers had Rodgers ranked far higher than No. 24 on their draft board. Green Bay also felt Rodgers was entering an ideal situation, one where he could watch and learn in a low-pressure environment. Then when Favre did eventually leave, Rodgers would have had ample time to prepare.

"I'm sure it was a long day for Aaron," Cal coach Jeff Tedford said on draft day. "People thought he would be one of the

Aaron Rodgers was all smiles after being selected by the Packers. Afterwards, he said, "I think it's going to be exciting. It's going to be a great fit."

first five picks, and it didn't work that way. A lot of teams didn't need quarterbacks. But if I know Aaron, he will take this as motivation. He's going to have talent around him, and there's not a better guy to learn the game from than Brett Favre."

At the end of the day, no one could determine exactly why Rodgers had plummeted that day. Some NFL personnel later said Rodgers had come across as too cocky during predraft interviews. Perhaps, but most teams also want a high level of confidence and self-assuredness from that position. What might have hurt Rodgers more than anything was the brutal track record of Tedford-coached quarterbacks. Several NFL executives simply figured Rodgers was next in line to flop.

The Packers most certainly didn't share that belief, though. "If there was a report that he was going to slip I would have been shocked," Bevell said. "I'm still in a little bit of a state of shock that he came down to us, and it's an exciting pick for us."

Tedford's quarterbacks were often called robotic, and because of their deliveries, they couldn't translate their collegiate success to the NFL. When Rodgers stepped out from under center as a collegian, he immediately brought the ball up near his earhole, which is about a foot higher than someone like Favre, who held the ball at shoulder length. The advantage to Rodgers' delivery was that the release is short and compact so he could get rid of the ball quickly. The drawback is that Rodgers didn't bring the ball back as far as other quarterbacks, so his strength on deeper passes was affected.

On draft day, Rodgers indicated he'd rather not mess with his throwing motion but said he'd adjust if told to. "I'm very coachable, so if the coaching staff here wants me to think about changing that up, I'll definitely be open to doing that," he said. "But unless I find a different way of throwing, I don't really feel like the way I throw is a negative. But I'm definitely open to suggestions."

As Rodgers entered the league, he did so at a position that faced long odds. Between 1982 and 2001 there were 37 quarterbacks taken in round one. By subjective count, 11 of those (Michael Vick, Donovan McNabb, Daunte Culpepper, Peyton Manning, Steve McNair, Drew Bledsoe, Troy

Aaron Rodgers, right, celebrates with his mother, Darla, and father, Ed, after being drafted by the Green Bay Packers.

Aikman, John Elway, Jim Kelly, Dan Marino, and Vinny Testaverde) proved more than worthy of their draft status. Another 11 (Bernie Kosar, Kerry Collins, Trent Dilfer, Chad Pennington, Chris Miller, Jim Harbaugh, Jim Everett, Tony Eason, Ken O'Brien, Jim McMahon, and Tommy Maddox) were solid pros. Finally, 15 others (Tim Couch, Akili Smith, Cade McNown, Ryan Leaf, Jim Druckenmiller, Heath Shuler, Rick Mirer, David Klingler, Todd Marinovich, Jeff George, Andre Ware, Kelly Stouffer, Chuck Long, Todd Blackledge, and Art Schlichter) were complete busts.

So, based on 20 years of history, the odds of Rodgers hitting it big were roughly 30 percent. "I didn't know that, but now I'm all depressed," Thompson said. "I don't know. I think a lot of times the urgency to get a quarterback and the importance of that position and plus there are so many things going on that make up a really good quarterback ... sometimes there's not that much difference between a really good quarterback and one that can't quite function amongst the chaos that happens once you snap the ball. I don't think you know that until you really have it. I think most of the quarterbacks who come from the first or the second round, sometimes from the sixth round as we know with Tom Brady, clearly it's not an exact science, but you try to make the best judgments you can. I haven't really thought about the failure or the success rate of the first-round quarterback."

Thompson certainly started thinking about it more that night, after making Rodgers his first-ever pick as Green Bay's general manager. Rodgers, on the other hand, was just happy his long day had ended. "I noticed looking at my watch a couple of times and hours were passing," he said. "We got excited a few times hoping that teams were going to take a chance on me. I got some calls from some friends, and I just tried to stay positive knowing that God had a plan for me where I didn't see where his hand was at the time, but now I know that he has had this plan for me since the beginning of time, and I'm excited to be a Packer."

The excitement was just beginning. ■

Aaron Rodgers holds up a Green Bay No. 1 jersey on draft day 2005. Little did anyone know that by Rodgers' sixth season, he and the Packers would be No. 1.

CHAPTER 4

THE UNDERSTUDY YEARS

When Aaron Rodgers arrived at Butte College back in the fall of 2002, he asked to wear No. 12, his old high school number. That was already taken, though, by a player named Shaun Bodiford who, ironically, Rodgers would later play with in Green Bay. Rodgers then asked for No. 8 because his boyhood hero, Steve Young, wore that number. But that was taken, too. Rodgers finally asked Butte coach Craig Rigsbee for No. 4. Why? "He told me, 'I just love how Brett Favre plays,'" Rigsbee said. "Pretty ironic." That's for sure.

Now, Favre and Rodgers were teammates, and things didn't get off to a stellar start. Rodgers arrived in Green Bay for his first mini-camp less than a week after he was drafted and immediately found himself in the middle of a firestorm. During an

interview with ESPN, Rodgers was asked his thoughts on Favre being given the camp off. His response? "Lazy," Rodgers quipped. While Rodgers' tongue was firmly planted in his cheek, some took the brash rookie's comment the wrong way.

At the time, Favre had started 205 consecutive games in Green Bay, a streak that would reach 253 by the time he left. And while Rodgers insisted he was joking, he immediately knew it was a bad joke. "That was a joke. It was definitely a joke," Rodgers said the next day. "Bad sense of humor. Brett's a phenomenal quarterback, and I just hope he didn't take it the wrong way because I was simply joking."

The relationship between Favre and Rodgers got off on the wrong foot, and it remained icy throughout. Rodgers simply wanted to learn from one of the NFL's

The relationship between Aaron Rodgers (right) and Brett Favre got off to a rough start and never got much better.

"HIS MECHANICS ARE (EXPLETIVE) UP. EVERYTHING HE THREW AT CAL WAS DINK AND DUNK STUFF. I SAW HIM THIS SUMMER, AND HE STUNK THE PLACE UP."

—AFC scouting director

best. But Favre viewed Rodgers as a threat and hated the fact that the Packers had his eventual replacement in house. Favre had no desire to tutor Rodgers. Instead, Favre was doing all he could to hang on.

During that first mini-camp, though, Rodgers showed he had miles to travel before becoming Favre's successor. The pinpoint accuracy and confidence he displayed at Cal were gone. Far too many of Rodgers' throws sailed high on him. And he was indecisive in his reads. Even though Rodgers' struggles were par for the rookie course, the Packers seemed concerned.

"Something is causing him to have his ball sail," offensive coordinator Tom Rossley said of Rodgers. "He's high on all of his throws. He's not really cutting loose, and he's not following through and finishing on the ball. I want to see him torque and throw the ball hard. I think then the ball will start coming out at a better trajectory."

Rodgers had posted impressive scores of 1,310 on his SATs and a 35 on the Wonderlic test. But after his first mini-camp, Rodgers admitted he was extremely overwhelmed. "I did throw a lot of high balls," Rodgers said that weekend. "I've always said you throw from the ground up, from your feet up. And when you're not confident in your reads, you're late on stuff, you rush stuff, your feet are out of position, and the ball goes high. And until I get my timing down on these plays, I will throw some high balls. My IQ's pretty high, and I am picking it up pretty fast. I think the coaches would say that as well. As far as calling the plays, that's getting better and better every day I'm getting better at that. I don't feel I'm playing terrible. But obviously I want to get better, and I'm excited about doing that."

It didn't happen for Rodgers that summer, either. During Rodgers' first training camp, he quarterbacked Green Bay's offense for 20 series against No. 2 and 3 defenses. On just one of those did Rodgers lead the Packers to any points. Throughout that summer, Rodgers won points for his pocket awareness, nifty feet, and terrific poise, which helped him survive behind a makeshift offensive line. Rodgers also showed more athleticism than many thought he possessed coming out of Cal. But too often, Rodgers settled for checkdowns instead of looking downfield.

The scouts that doubted Rodgers on draft day had even more questions now. They wondered if Rodgers had an NFL-caliber arm. They questioned if Rodgers' big numbers at Cal came largely from the quarterback-friendly system employed by Jeff Tedford. And ultimately, many doubted if he could someday replace Favre. "I was never a Rodgers guy from the start," one AFC college scouting director said before the 2005 season began. "His mechanics are (expletive) up. Everything he threw at Cal was dink and dunk

stuff. I saw him this summer, and he stunk the place up." When summer ended, many wondered if Rodgers deserved the No. 2 spot instead of veteran Craig Nall. The previous season, Nall had posted a lights-out passer rating of 139.4 while occasionally relieving Favre.

But when the regular season began, Rodgers was named No. 2. And while the move may have been political, Rodgers did all he could to prove it was the right choice. "I'm just starting to climb to my potential," Rodgers insisted. "I feel real confident, and I'm making good steps. I'm getting better each day. I feel more confident, more comfortable in the pocket and in this offense. Obviously, we've got to execute a little better and make some plays when we get the opportunity. I've got to put the ball in better spots, but I felt good about making plays outside the pocket when the pocket broke down. And I just think I'm going to keep getting better."

Rodgers didn't change a lot of minds during the regular season, though. The 2005 campaign was a miserable one in Green Bay. The Packers were ravaged by injury, began the year 0–4, and were just 2–10 in early December. Favre was struggling through a brutal season, one in which he'd eventually throw 29 interceptions and just 20 touchdowns. Many fans began clamoring for Rodgers, to see if a few months of watching had helped the No. 1 draft pick.

But Mike Sherman, who was stripped of his general manager duties the previous offseason and would be fired as head coach after the season, had no interest in what Rodgers could do. Remember, Sherman never wanted Rodgers in the first place. He wanted some help for a leaky defense or a new offensive weapon for Favre. The last thing Sherman wanted general manager Ted Thompson to do was draft a quarterback to sit on the bench.

So when the Packers bottomed out that year, Sherman certainly wasn't going to turn things over to a player he didn't want in the first place. "I can't see not playing to win a game," Sherman said. "I think that's what we're supposed to do. We're going to play to win."

Considering Rodgers had shown very little at that point, the Packers themselves certainly weren't arguing. "I'm just going to put it to you this way," veteran right tackle Mark Tauscher said. "(Favre's) a great quarterback. I don't think there's

Facing constant media scrutiny, Aaron Rodgers struggled immensely during his first mini-camp and first training camp in Green Bay.

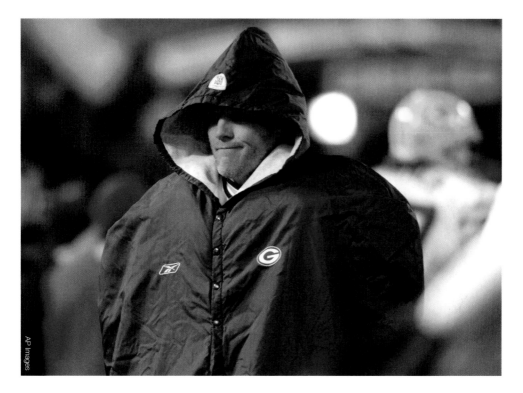

AP Images

been any slip in his game, his play has kept us competitive, and he's done everything in his power to make this team win. So why would you take away your best weapon and put in someone with no experience and so much youth?

"There's time to develop guys, and times to try and win games. You don't develop guys to win games. You try to win every game you play, and if you don't try to win every game you play, then you're in the wrong business. You're here to win. I think Brett's playing as good as he's ever played. He's still one of the best quarterbacks in this league, and he makes plays that no other player can make. If you're going to put your best player on the bench, I don't know what kind of sense that makes. I think it's insane to even bring it up."

So Rodgers' rookie season ended like it began: with a whimper. He relieved Favre in three games and went 9-of-16 for 65 yards. Rodgers didn't throw a touchdown, had one interception, and put up a paltry quarterback rating of 39.8. One season in, Rodgers was still being billed as the heir apparent to Favre. His play, though, didn't exactly win anybody over.

So after Green Bay's dreadful season had concluded, the Packers were all crossing

Brett Favre had a rough 2005 season, but the Packers never gave serious consideration to sitting him and playing Aaron Rodgers.

their fingers that Favre would come back in 2006 and Rodgers could continue developing. "I think Aaron will be fine when he gets his chance," wideout Donald Driver said that year. "Now hopefully, he doesn't get that chance for a while. The best thing that could happen is for Brett to come back, because that man still has a lot of football in him. Then Aaron could keep learning and be even more prepared when his chance comes along."

The 2006 offseason was a tumultuous one in tiny Green Bay. Sherman was fired one day after the Packers' season finale. Ten days later, Mike McCarthy—who was San Francisco's offensive coordinator when the 49ers passed on Rodgers—was hired as the 14th head coach in Green Bay history. And after Jeff Jagodzinski was brought in as offensive coordinator and Tom Clements was hired to coach quarterbacks, Rodgers was suddenly working with an entirely new staff.

Whereas Sherman and his staff had elected not to mess with Rodgers' carriage, McCarthy's staff slowly tinkered with his release point. Instead of that mechanical motion where Rodgers was throwing the ball

In Aaron Rodgers' first season in Green Bay, he played in just three games and had a paltry passer rating of 39.8.

> ## "I'M THE BACKUP TO ONE OF THE GREATEST QUARTERBACKS OF ALL TIME, AND I KNOW THAT UNTIL HE'S READY TO CALL IT QUITS, BE IT END OF THIS YEAR, END OF NEXT YEAR, END OF THE YEAR AFTER THAT, I KNOW MY ROLE. —Aaron Rodgers

from the ear hole of his helmet, McCarthy gradually lowered the delivery. Suddenly, Rodgers' throwing motion looked more natural and effortless.

From the start of training camp that summer, Rodgers was a different player. Some of it had to do with his improved delivery. But much of it was the simple fact that Rodgers now understood his playbook from A to Z. Instead of thinking, Rodgers was simply playing football again. "He's comfortable and that's the whole thing," wideout Donald Driver said. "When you're comfortable in the offense, it makes it easier to just go and play. He's more comfortable and more relaxed and much better than he was last year."

That showed throughout Rodgers'

breakthrough summer. Rodgers finished the preseason with a quarterback rating of 101.1 and led Green Bay's No. 2 offense to 24 points in 22 possessions. A year earlier, Rodgers had a paltry quarterback rating of 53.0 in the preseason. "I think it went a lot better," Rodgers said of his 2006 preseason. "We put some points on the board. Overall, I think it was a good experience, and I got a lot better. The offseason work definitely paid off. We'll see how it goes."

In four preseason games, Rodgers completed 22 of 38 passes (57.9 percent) for 323 yards. He threw three touchdowns, had one interception, averaged 8.5 yards per pass attempt, and lost two fumbles. In the 22 series Rodgers conducted, he led the Packers to 25 first downs, and Green

Chico Enterprise-Record/Jason Halley

Bay averaged 5.0 net yards per play.

A year earlier, Rodgers was 20-of-37 (54.1 percent) for 172 yards, an average of just 4.65 yards per passing attempt. He threw two interceptions, one touchdown, and was admittedly lost at times. "What's the difference between this year and last year?" Rodgers asked. "Comfort level, knowledge of the offense, confidence. I feel like I'm a much better player than I was last year. Obviously, that won't bear a lot of fruit until I have a chance to be a starter, but I feel good about where I'm at after preseason camp No. 2."

Rodgers was generally more consistent in practice each day, as well. In 11-on-11 drills, he completed 165 of 263 passes (62.7 percent) with seven interceptions. In 7-on-7 drills, he was 102-of- 159 (64.2 percent) with two picks. "He's getting better," Packers coach Mike McCarthy said of Rodgers. "You're looking at a guy who's going to mature. He's got athletic ability that people still haven't seen. He's confident and has a really good understanding of what's going on. I just think from the film I watched last year, he's really improved. He has a chance to be a really good player."

Rodgers also showed more arm strength than he had as a rookie. And he

Aaron Rodgers chats with (left to right) his agent Michael Sullivan, his father, Ed, his brothers, Luke and Jordan, and his mother, Darla, after the Packers beat the 49ers 30–19 in San Francisco on December 10, 2006.

displayed an adept touch on the deep ball, something that certainly caught the eye of his teammates and coaches. "You've always got to want to play and improve," Rodgers said. "I think if you're content with being a backup, you're not going to last long in this league, although obviously I know my role on this team.

"I'm the backup to one of the greatest quarterbacks of all time, and I know that until he's ready to call it quits, be it end of this year, end of next year, end of the year after that, I know my role. But at the same time, the attitude I have to have is one of mainly working on things to get better and always looking for ways to improve." Unfortunately for Rodgers, once the season started, he had to look awfully hard for ways to keep getting better. Favre had a bounce-back year in 2006, and Rodgers saw precious little time on Sundays.

To Rodgers' credit, though, his day-to-day consistency was a real strength. Rodgers made the most of his limited repetitions in practice, he continued to master the offense through film study, and he became a popular figure in the Packers'

locker room. "He practices like he's ready," Green Bay tight end Bubba Franks said. "You never know until you put him in, but he's practicing like he's the starter, which has got to give him a little confidence. The coach lets him go with the (No.) 1s, and he gets good reps. But right now, no one's sure how he'll do until he gets out there and does it."

Rodgers saw action in just two games that season and struggled. He finished with a 48.2 passer rating after completing just six of 15 passes for 46 yards and didn't have an interception or touchdown pass. The most frustrating afternoon of Rodgers' season came during a 35–0 home loss to mighty New England in late November. Favre left the game late in the first half with an elbow injury and the Packers trailing 21–0.

Rodgers had a chance to show the fan base what the future might look like. Instead, they had to be longing for the past after Rodgers went just 4-of-12 for 32 yards, took three sacks, and fumbled once. "I think I put him in a tough situation trying to get out there and throw the ball

Aaron Rodgers rolls out to pass during a 2006 preseason game against the Titans. Rodgers rarely left the sideline during the 2006 regular season. He played in just two games and had a 48.2 passer rating.

every time," McCarthy said. "I thought sometimes he got out of the offense, but I thought he made some plays with his feet. I think you see his athletic ability. It was a great test for his preparation, how important it is for the backup quarterback to prepare harder and more than the starter. ... He was put in a tough spot."

Adding injury to insult, Rodgers suffered a broken foot and spent the final six weeks of the regular season on injured reserve. "He's got talent, he has ability, he has know-how," McCarthy insisted of Rodgers. "When his opportunity comes, I want to put my foot on the gas and go with him. The only thing you don't know with a quarterback until he gets a chance is if he can lead your offense."

Still, as Rodgers' second season in Green Bay came to a close, the jury was still out. Rodgers had improved immensely during an impressive summer. But that didn't carry over to his brief playing opportunities in the regular season. And now, two years into his young career, Rodgers' passer rating was a paltry 43.9.

"All I can do is keep working hard," Rodgers said. "I think guys respect someone that comes to work every day and puts his heart and soul into this, and I think I do. And even though I'm not playing, I think guys see my enthusiasm, the way I care about the guys and cheerlead for other guys, and they respect that. And when my time comes, I'll be ready." Per usual, the Packers had no idea when that time would be.

Green Bay closed the regular season with a bang, winning its final four games and improving to 8–8. After the season finale in Chicago that year, Favre cried on national television, giving many the impression he'd retire. So as the Packers exited Green Bay that January, they had no idea if the Rodgers' era would start in 2007. Just in case, Green Bay's brass was putting on a brave face.

"I think Aaron Rodgers is a young man that has excellent ability," McCarthy said. "Mentally he has an excellent understanding and the ability to comprehend and communicate our system. I think he's done a very good job in the time we've been together in preparing himself, going

By 2007, Aaron Rodgers was playing like a No. 1 draft pick...but Brett Favre's high level of play left Rodgers wearing a headset for most of the season.

through quarterback school last year. We'll take the same path this year, so I look for him to improve."

Just how much—and how soon—depended largely on Favre.

• •

Legendary UCLA basketball coach John Wooden had several axioms for life. Among them were the following:

• Flexibility is the key to stability.
• Failure to prepare is preparing to fail.
• Be quick, but don't hurry.

All would have been applicable to Rodgers in the 2007 season.

By Year 3 of his apprenticeship under Favre, Rodgers felt like he was ready to lead the Packers. But after the Packers closed the 2006 season with four straight wins, Favre took just four weeks—a relatively short amount of time for him—to declare he'd be back for a 16th season in Green Bay. The previous offseason, Favre had waited until April to announce he'd be back.

"I am so excited about coming back," Favre said. "We have a good nucleus of young players. We were 8–8 last year, and that's encouraging. My offensive line looks good, the defense played good down the stretch. I'm excited about playing for a talented young football team."

Publicly, Rodgers said all the right things. But deep down, Rodgers believed he was ready to take over. He proved it again that summer by lighting it up during training camp. Rodgers got several chances to play with the No. 1 offense during preseason games that summer, and for the most part, he shined.

In Green Bay's second preseason game against Seattle, Rodgers was 5-of-7 for 58 yards, one TD, and a 135.7 quarterback rating while working with the first-team offense. One week later against Jacksonville, Rodgers was 5-of-7 for 71 yards, zero TDs, and a 103.9 rating when leading the No. 1s.

"I'm not trying to be glib, but I've liked him all along," Packers general manager Ted Thompson said of Rodgers. "Yeah, he went through some tough times, but preseason games and that sort of thing, and even the game he played in last year, I don't think necessarily is the telling tale. I

Aaron Rodgers and Brett Favre looked loose during this 2007 practice, but neither knew that they faced a tense transition in the months ahead.

> ## "I THINK HE'S A YOUNG MAN THAT'S CONFIDENT, THAT'S SMART, THAT IS PHYSICALLY TALENTED, THAT BELIEVES HE CAN PLAY, AND HE HAS UNDERSTOOD AND ACCEPTED THE ROLE THAT HE'S IN, EVEN THOUGH HE STILL WANTS TO PLAY. I'M PROUD OF THE WAY HE CARRIES HIMSELF."

—Ted Thompson

think he's a young man that's confident, that's smart, that is physically talented, that believes he can play, and he has understood and accepted the role that he's in, even though he still wants to play. I'm proud of the way he carries himself. I think he's going to be a good player, and I'm pleased with the way he's playing now."

By the time summer ended, it was apparent Green Bay had an extremely gifted second-string quarterback. The uncertain, hesitant, indecisive player of 2005 was gone. Now, Rodgers was playing fast, confident, and with total certainty. "Confidence wise, it probably hasn't wavered that much," Rodgers said. "But comfort wise, I think that's the most important thing. Now for me, I'm confident and comfortable within the offense, and I just feel like the game is able to slow down for me. I'm able to go through my progressions ... and for me it's just getting to a comfort level. And I feel like I'm getting closer to that."

Rodgers finished that summer with a passer rating of 98.3, threw three TDs, and had no interceptions. But when the season began, it was back to watching and waiting. And what Rodgers watched was a brilliant season by Favre and the Packers. Green Bay began the year 10–1, and Favre was playing at an MVP level. "All I can do is keep practicing hard, keep studying, and if I do get the chance to play, just go out

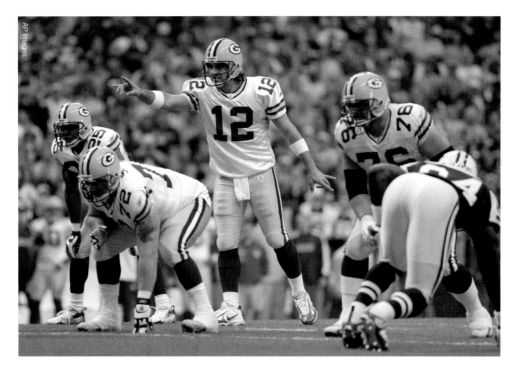

there and make the most of it," Rodgers said that November.

Shockingly, that chance came in Green Bay's biggest regular season game in a decade. Surprisingly, Rodgers was the star. Green Bay went to Dallas for a battle of 10–1 teams, where the winner had a clear inside track to homefield advantage throughout the NFC playoffs. Favre struggled miserably, threw two early interceptions, and then exited with an elbow injury and the Packers in a 27–10 hole.

With 9 minutes, 53 seconds left in the second quarter, Rodgers entered the huddle of what had been a lifeless offense. The Packers were down three scores, and little

had gone right. Over the next two-plus hours, Rodgers showed Packer Nation there might indeed be life after Favre.

On the Packers' second possession with Rodgers in charge, he engineered an 8-play, 74-yard touchdown drive that pulled Green Bay to within 27–17 at halftime. Wideout Greg Jennings made the play of the drive by taking a short out route and turning it into a 43-yard gain. Rodgers and Jennings then hooked up for an 11-yard TD just 31 seconds before halftime.

On Green Bay's first drive of the second half, Rodgers was back at it again. This time, he led a 12-play, 69-yard march that pulled the Packers to within 27–24. "To

Rodgers impressed a national television audience with a gutsy November 2007 performance against the Cowboys in relief of an injured Favre. Green Bay may have lost the game but the team discovered its future starter.

me, Aaron Rodgers played way better than Brett Favre," Cowboys linebacker Bradie James said afterward. "Brett Favre was just throwing the ball up. I don't know if we'd rather have him in there or Rodgers."

Green Bay never could get over the hump and fell, 37–27, in a game that eventually gave the Cowboys the NFC's top seed. But Rodgers won a lot of people over with his performance that night. He finished the game 18-of-26 for 201 yards, his first NFL touchdown, and an impressive quarterback rating of 104.8.

"I just can't say enough about his preparation, because I didn't even blink," Packers coach Mike McCarthy said of Rodgers. "I didn't throw anything out. I've been in that position before when you have to go to your backup or go to your third guy or even your fourth guy. I went through it in San Francisco, and you just start crossing plays off the chart, and that wasn't the case. I thought Aaron did an excellent job."

Even Favre—who was far from the ideal mentor—sang Rodgers' praises afterward. "I thought he played great," Favre said of Rodgers. "He gave us a chance to win. I thought he was ready to play. I was hoping it would be in different circumstances ... but I thought he did a fine job."

While Rodgers answered many questions that night, more were soon to arise. The week after the Dallas game, Rodgers suffered a hamstring injury in practice and was inactive the final four weeks of the regular season. That marked the second straight season Rodgers missed substantial time, and many wondered if he could stay on the field.

Of course, the way Favre was going that season, it didn't matter much. Favre finished that regular season with 28 touchdowns, 15 interceptions, and a passer rating of 95.7. Green Bay went 13–3, earned the No. 2 seed in the postseason, and Favre finished second in the MVP voting to New England's Tom Brady.

"I just think he's doing a great job of running the offense," McCarthy said of Favre late that season. "We've asked him to do some things. We've asked him to do more of things that he hasn't had to do a lot of in the past. I'm talking more spread offense and taking advantage of [things] at the line-of-scrimmage situations. So he's done a very good job."

The Packers defeated Seattle in the

NFC Divisional Game that season, 42–20. But their year ended in heartbreak with a 23–20 overtime loss to the visiting New York Giants in the NFC Championship Game. Favre struggled that night, and his overtime interception led to a game-winning field goal by the Giants' Lawrence Tynes. Still, as the Packers left that offseason, no one expected the 38-year-old Favre to call it quits. He was still playing at an elite level, the Packers were one game from the Super Bowl, and their future was remarkably bright.

"I said, 'You going to give me one more year?' He just kind of giggled," wideout Greg Jennings said. "I did the same thing last year, and he said, 'We'll see,' and he was back. Who knows? Hopefully he's back. We'd definitely like to see him in that locker over there one more time." Rodgers himself expected Favre back. And when Rodgers left Lambeau Field that frigid January night, he still had no idea what his own future in Green Bay held.

Little did Rodgers know that his future was soon to be filled with drama, drama, and more drama. ■

Aaron Rodgers (left) and Brett Favre became closer during the 2007 season, but that was all about to change during the crazy summer of 2008.

CHAPTER 5

A MESSY TRANSITION

It was March 4, 2008, and Aaron Rodgers' life had just gotten a whole lot crazier. By 7:00 AM that day, Rodgers had received eight phone calls. Could it be? Apparently it could. Brett Favre was set to call it quits. The Green Bay Packers were now officially Rodgers' team.

"I'm in a good situation, I've got a great team around me," Rodgers said shortly after news of Favre's retirement broke. "A lot of people have been focusing on what I'm going to do. It's what the team is going to do, really. I'm an important part of that, and I know my role. I need to play well, and I'm not really going to have a grace period either. The expectations that people are going to have are very high. The expectations I have of myself are very high as well. I've definitely been told there haven't been a lot of guys

following a legend that play well. Hopefully I'll have like a Steve Young kind of experience here."

Rodgers, a passionate San Francisco 49ers fan as a child, watched closely when Young replaced the legendary Joe Montana in 1992. Although Young eventually guided the 49ers to a championship in Super Bowl XXIX, not all San Francisco fans were rejoicing. "I know a lot of friends and family who were Joe Montana fans who it didn't matter how good Steve Young did," Rodgers said. "They weren't going to cheer for him because he wasn't Joe Montana."

In many ways, Rodgers could relate. Rodgers' three-year waiting period had at times felt like 30. Those three seasons, though, had given Rodgers an opportunity to learn the intricacies of Green Bay's

Green Bay Packers quarterback Brett Favre gets choked up when announcing his retirement on March 6, 2008.

> # "IF (FANS) WANT ME TO BE THE NEXT BRETT FAVRE, I'M NOT GOING TO BE HIM. I'M AARON RODGERS. THAT'S WHO I AM. I'M GOING TO BE THE BEST QUARTERBACK I CAN BE. HE DID IT HIS WAY, AND I'M GOING TO DO IT MY WAY. —Aaron Rodgers"

offense, study defenses, and pick up some tricks from Favre. Much of Packer Nation, though, was devastated by the news of Favre's departure. Green Bay's iconic quarterback had been brilliant in 2007 and most expected Favre back in 2008.

To those fans looking for the nearest bridge, Rodgers had the following message. "I'm not Brett Favre," Rodgers said. "If [fans] want me to be the next Brett Favre, I'm not going to be him. I'm Aaron Rodgers. That's who I am. I'm going to be the best quarterback I can be. He did it his way, and I'm going to do it my way, and hopefully I can be successful."

Despite Rodgers' minimal game experience, the Packers were remarkably confident moving forward with him. In fact, at the 2008 NFL Combine, one Packers assistant coach said he believed Green Bay would have won the Super Bowl in '07 if Rodgers had been the starter. No one will ever know that answer, but Rodgers had become far more comfortable with the NFL game since arriving, something he showed during that stellar performance in Dallas in 2007. Rodgers had also formed a tight bond with several teammates, earned the respect of the locker room, and tried becoming a leader.

"I like the fact that he has come into a situation that is difficult, and he has taken on those responsibilities," Packers general manager Ted Thompson said. "The fans haven't seen him, but he goes out to practice every day, he's very well received by his teammates, he and Brett got along well, he understood his role. That's a difficult thing to do for a young man that wants to play. So, I think he's positioned

himself as a leader even though he wasn't playing, and I think he's positioned himself to be a leader going forward."

Packers coach Mike McCarthy echoed Thompson's sentiments. "I have zero concerns about Aaron Rodgers," McCarthy said. "I think his time is now. He's ready to go, and he will have another offseason to prepare for that. We need to make sure that we're ready for the whole quarterback position, and that is our focus."

Rodgers had been preparing throughout the offseason as though he'd be Favre's backup for a fourth straight year. But in the blink of an eye, Rodgers went from obscurity to the spotlight. "I'm always going to be compared to Brett, obviously," Rodgers said. "I think I just need to be my own quarterback, be my own man.

"And I think the most important thing ... to me was the texts I got from my teammates—just the encouragement. I've always felt like they believe in me just because they see my work ethic. But just to have that reinforced by some of the text messages and calls I got was pretty special."

In the months ahead, Rodgers probably thought back to many of those messages. Because things inside Green Bay's organization were about to get a whole lot messier.

• •

April and May came with barely a whimper in tiny Green Bay. On April 25, the Packers placed Favre on the reserve-retired list and announced plans to retire his No. 4 jersey in the regular-season opener against Minnesota. During April's NFL Draft, the Packers used a second-round pick on quarterback Brian Brohm of Louisville. The Packers later used a seventh rounder on quarterback Matt Flynn of LSU.

Those picks were made largely for depth, though, as the Packers didn't have another quarterback on the roster. "Mike said I'm the guy. Ted said I'm the guy," Rodgers said when asked if he might have to battle Brohm for the starting job. "Brian looks like he's a good player. He's smart, he's picking up the offense pretty well. But it's really in my hands. If I play well, everything's going to take care of itself. And if I don't, either Brian or somebody else will be replacing me, and I'll know before anybody else."

Of that trio, Rodgers truly had little to worry about. Brohm was overmatched

from day one and lasted just one season in Green Bay. Flynn performed far better than a typical seventh-round draft choice, but he was light years behind Rodgers.

Clearly, this was Rodgers' team now. And when Green Bay gathered for its first organized team activity session in May, Rodgers was the clear-cut starter and downright giddy about the opportunity that awaited. "It feels great," Rodgers said. "I've taken the No. 1 reps in practice throughout the last three years, but to know that I'm the guy going into the season is pretty exciting, because guys are starting to rally around my leadership style and the way I do things. Like I said, I've been waiting for this experience, this opportunity, my whole life, so it's pretty exciting."

Many of Rodgers' teammates shared that excitement. "It's becoming a catch phrase, but we're all excited," left guard Daryn Colledge said. "Everyone misses Brett. Everyone loves Brett and his humor and all that. But we're such a young team that I think there's just a ton of excitement out there right now. There's kind of a buzz right now, and we

want to prove everybody wrong.

"We don't want to be that team that was 13–3 and then doesn't make the playoffs. We want to build a dynasty. We want to do it with Aaron. I think he's going to bring a whole different dynamic than Brett. He's the kind of guy that most guys will definitely go to battle for."

That spring, Rodgers was a different quarterback from the one who arrived in Green Bay three years earlier. He had lowered his body fat and was in the best physical shape of his life. Rodgers no longer held the ball near his ear like he did back in 2005. And McCarthy had worked extensively on Rodgers' footwork with terrific results.

"I think he's gotten better, no question," Packers offensive coordinator Joe Philbin said. "He was a young guy still ... and there's no question he's improved. He moves well and fluidly. He's a fluid athlete. He's throwing some competitive balls down the field."

He sure was. That entire spring, Rodgers was throwing the ball with more power and accuracy than any time since

his arrival in Green Bay. Rodgers' arm strength had been questioned before the NFL Draft in 2005, which is one reason he slid to No. 24 that year. But watching Rodgers hum balls around the Don Hutson Center that May and June, you had to wonder how so many NFL scouts could be wrong.

"He could always throw the ball. I was at his college workout, and his arm strength was never a factor in my opinion," said McCarthy, who was one of the people who passed on Rodgers during that 2005 draft. "But I definitely do think he throws it probably better now than he did; just overall his body, his conditioning, and his strength have improved. I would say he does throw maybe with more velocity than he initially did. Aaron Rodgers has a strong arm, always has in my experience with him."

Still, most national "experts" were predicting failure for Rodgers. Of course, all they had to judge Rodgers on was seven career games, in which his passer rating was 73.3. But Rodgers was doing all he could to ignore the critics. "I try not to [pay attention]," Rodgers said. "I watch *Lost* and *The Office* when I watch TV. But I have a lot of friends, and that stuff means a lot to them so I hear just about everything that anybody says. "My family and I, we've had conversations about not worrying about what other people say about me. Because the only people whose opinions I really care about, no disrespect to anybody in the media, are the 53 guys in the locker room, our personnel department, our coaching staff."

By the end of mini-camps that June, the Packers were confident in what they had. Rodgers had done all they'd hoped, and Green Bay's coaching staff felt extremely confident they could build on their 2007 successes. "I've been setting myself up mentally for this for a while," Rodgers said. "It's exciting, it really is, to know that I'm going to get first shot, that I'm the guy, and really my own destiny is in my hands. If I play well, everything is going to take care of itself."

Or would it? On June 20—the final day of offseason practices—McCarthy took a call from Favre, who told his coach

"HE COULD ALWAYS THROW THE BALL. I WAS AT HIS COLLEGE WORKOUT, AND HIS ARM STRENGTH WAS NEVER A FACTOR IN MY OPINION. —Mike McCarthy

he still had an "itch" to play and wanted back in. "When he picked up the phone again after he dropped it, he said, 'Oh, God, Brett. You're putting us in a tight spot,'" Favre later said of his conversation with McCarthy. "He said, 'Brett, playing here is not an option.' Those were his exact, exact words."

What had been a quiet three months in Green Bay had just gotten a whole lot louder. And things were only getting started.

Green Bay's players soon went off for some R&R before training camp. Favre and the Packers, though, turned their saga into a nightly soap opera. Favre continued to tell the Packers he wanted to come back. Green Bay's decision makers continued to tell him no. Both sides made their stances very public, and Rodgers had no choice but to watch it all play out.

"I realized back in 2005 that the only things I need to worry about are the things I can control," Rodgers said. "And I can't control the decision that the organization makes, or Brett's decisions. So I can control my preparation and my effort and my focus, and that's what I'm trying to do." Still, the constant back and forth was brutal for all parties.

On July 8, Favre met with McCarthy and Thompson and expressed a strong desire to play. The Packers' brass tried talking Favre out of that decision. On July 11, Favre asked the Packers for his release so he could return to the NFL with another team. Green Bay, believing that Favre wanted to return to the NFC North with either Minnesota or Chicago, denied his request.

"The finality of his decision to retire was accepted by the organization," the Packers said in a team statement. "At that point, the Green Bay Packers made the commitment to move forward with our football team." On July 17, the Packers accused the Vikings of tampering, something

that was never proven. Favre did not show up for the start of training camp on July 27, but two days later he faxed his official request for reinstatement to the NFL.

Day after day, Rodgers was bombarded by a bevy of questions—and very few were about anything happening on the field. "I don't need people to feel sorry for me," Rodgers said. "Playing quarterback is a tough job, and there's a lot of scrutiny that goes along with that. You get too much blame a lot of times; you get too much credit a lot of times. And you just have to stay balanced and stay even-keeled. The last three years and this offseason have made me the person I am today, and I wouldn't have changed it for anything."

On July 30, Packers president Mark Murphy flew to Mississippi and offered Favre a lucrative marketing deal to stay retired: 10 years, $20 million. Favre rejected the offer and flew to Green Bay on July 31. Two nights later, during the Packers' annual "Family Night" scrimmage at Lambeau Field, Rodgers heard a mixture of boos and cheers when he was introduced. "Yeah, I take it personally," Rodgers said. "But like I said, it's not the first time, and it won't be the last time."

With Favre's shadow looming large, Rodgers struggled that night, missing six straight passes at one point and throwing an interception to safety Aaron Rouse.

One day later, NFL Commissioner Roger Goodell reinstated Favre, and it appeared the Packers would hold an open competition for the quarterback job. "I'm a competitor. I'm going to compete," Rodgers said. "This isn't going to be easy. It's going to be a dogfight. And I know if they do open it up to competition, not a lot of people give me a chance, but I believe in myself, and I'm going to be the best I can be and let coach decide from there."

McCarthy insisted that he still hadn't made up his mind about how to proceed. "There have been no promises," McCarthy said. "Once again, there has been indecision throughout Brett's path back here to Green Bay. It's important for us to sit down and communicate."

Over the next two days, Favre and McCarthy met for nearly six hours in what McCarthy termed "brutally honest conversations. When it was over, the two sides agreed that it was better if Favre didn't remain with the Packers. "The train has left the station, whatever analogy you want,"

> # "IT WAS A DIFFICULT SITUATION.... BUT THE WHOLE TIME THE ORGANIZATION STOOD BY ME, AND THEY TOLD THE TRUTH, AND I TOLD THE TRUTH, AND WE MOVED ON TOGETHER."
> ## —Aaron Rodgers

McCarthy said. "He needs to jump on the train, and let's go. Or, if we can't get past things that have happened, I have to keep the train moving."

So on August 5, Favre flew home to Mississippi, and the next day he was traded to the New York Jets for a third-round draft choice. "This is, in many ways, sad that this is where it came to," Thompson said. "At the end of the day though, I think all parties involved felt like it was the best solution to a very difficult situation."

Finally, once and for all, the Packers were Rodgers' team. He had played the role of good soldier well through all the chaos, saying all the right things and never losing faith that he would keep the starting job the organization handed him months earlier. "It was a difficult situation," Rodgers said. "It was tough to stand up every day in front of the media not knowing what questions were coming at me and how the fans were going to react that day in practice. But the whole time the organization stood by me, and they told the truth, and I told the truth, and we moved on together.

"I think they knew what kind of person they were getting, and at the same time I hope they knew what kind of player they were getting as well. It gave me a lot of confidence that they stood by me through everything that happened. It was a trying time for myself and the organization, but the fact that they continued to stand by me and believe in me was definitely big for my confidence."

Rodgers had won half the battle: keeping his job. Now came the harder part: winning football games. ∎

Two days after Brett Favre's retirement press conference, Aaron Rodgers spoke confidently about leading the Packers into the future.

CHAPTER 6

A NEW STARTER IN GREEN BAY

The rest of that crazy summer of 2008 went without incident. The Packers were 1–3 that preseason, but Rodgers played at a high level throughout. He finished with a 103.6 passer rating and had the backing of his teammates. "Nothing changes," wideout Donald Driver said. "We don't do anything different than we've been doing when Brett was here. The play calling is going to stay the same. Cadence is going to stay the same. Nothing different. You just see a different face, and we all move on. And I think that's the big thing with us."

Still, the Favre-a-palooza had dragged on for more than a month and turned much of Green Bay's preseason into a circus. Needless to say, the Packers were excited for the regular season to begin. "Can't wait," wideout Greg Jennings said. "It's really been a long summer. Can't wait to get going."

Neither could Rodgers, who anxiously awaited his first NFL start. Fittingly, it came against NFC North rival Minnesota, a team that had geared its entire offseason around catching Green Bay. And the entire football world would be watching, as Packers-Vikings was being shown on Monday Night Football.

Roughly an hour before kickoff, Rodgers plopped down next to wideout Ruvell Martin inside the Green Bay Packers locker room. Rodgers was about to become the first quarterback not named Brett Favre to start a game for Green Bay in nearly 16 years. He was set to replace a living legend and the finest player in franchise history. And he was trying to win over a fan base that was still largely bitter over Favre's departure.

Aaron Rodgers was outstanding in the 2008 preseason, then led the Packers past the Minnesota Vikings in his first-ever career start.

"**HE PLAYED GREAT, MADE GOOD DECISIONS, AND I THINK HE WON THE RESPECT OF A LOT OF PEOPLE. I THINK A LOT OF PEOPLE HAVE MORE FAITH IN HIM NOW.** —Korey Hall"

So clearly, Rodgers was bouncing off the walls, right? "No," said Martin, who was Rodgers' best friend on the team. "He was calm as can be." Which is how Rodgers proceeded to play.

Rodgers certainly didn't make anyone forget Favre during his first NFL start. But he was efficient, accurate, and managed the game extremely well as the Packers notched a huge 24–19 win at Lambeau Field. Rodgers finished the night 18-of-22 for 178 yards, threw for a touchdown, ran for another, and posted a passer rating of 115.5. He also rushed for 35 yards and wasn't sacked a single time.

"It feels great," Rodgers said on a night when he was among the last to leave the Packers' locker room. "You've got to remind yourself it's just one win, but it was a big one. I think the talk this week was a lot about the Vikings and I don't think enough about the kind of team that we had. So we definitely wanted to play well tonight, and I think we did."

With all eyes focused on Rodgers, he certainly did his part. All Rodgers had to do in his first start was fill the shoes of the NFL's all-time leader in passing yards, touchdowns, and wins. Making things even more uncomfortable for Rodgers was the fact that Favre had excelled in his New York Jets debut with a passer rating of 125.9.

But Rodgers never blinked. For the most part, he kept his passes short and simple. The Packers used more max protection than in 2007, largely to slow Minnesota's vaunted pass rush. And Rodgers took very few chances in the passing game. Still, he did enough to lift his team to a huge win.

"He did what he had to do," Vikings

cornerback Cedric Griffin said of Rodgers. "Nothing special. Nothing great. But he executed real well, and they won the game. Congratulations to him." Minnesota linebacker Chad Greenway agreed. "I'd say he did his thing," Greenway said. "He didn't kill us, but he kept the chains moving and kind of picked away at us. He was efficient." That he was.

Green Bay's offense was brutal early on, some of it the fault of Rodgers, but much the responsibility of a reworked offensive line. The Packers had five first quarter penalties—all on the offensive line—and managed just 43 yards of total offense. Rodgers and Green Bay's attack finally got going in the second quarter, though, when they went to work on Minnesota's suspect passing defense.

On the Packers' first play of the second quarter, Rodgers unleashed a bomb for Jennings. Green Bay's top wideout adjusted nicely and made a 56-yard reception in front of Minnesota reserve corner Charles Gordon at the Minnesota 6-yard line. That set up a 1-yard TD pass from Rodgers to fullback Korey Hall on third-and-goal that gave the Packers a 7–3 lead.

"You know, I don't think he could have handled this whole situation better,"

Hall later said of Rodgers. "You can't imagine the amount of pressure he has on his shoulders right now, and he went out and was collected and calm. He played great, made good decisions, and I think he won the respect of a lot of people. I think a lot of people have more faith in him now. I think he's going to have a great season."

Later in the second quarter, Rodgers engineered an 8-play, 63-yard march that set up a 42-yard Mason Crosby field goal and gave Green Bay a 10–3 advantage. At halftime, Rodgers had completed 75 percent of his 16 attempts for 139 yards, with a passer rating of 121.6.

Rodgers wasn't asked to do much in the second half, thanks to a 76-yard punt return for a TD by Will Blackmon and a 57-yard run by Ryan Grant to the Vikings' 2-yard line. Grant's burst set Rodgers up for a 1-yard TD that made it 24–12 and provided what proved to be the game-winning points. "I thought Aaron Rodgers played well," Packers coach Mike McCarthy said afterward. "Number one, I thought he managed the game ... I thought he did a good job managing the game without taking chances. Playing with the play call and taking what the defense gave you and so forth. So I was pleased with his performance tonight."

Afterward, Rodgers knew this was nothing more than a start. There were still 15 games remaining, and no one was mentioning Rodgers in the same breath with Favre. But Rodgers' first impression certainly was a favorable one. "It was good to get the first one under your belt and move forward now," he said. "It was a huge game for us. That's what it was made out to be, and I feel like it was. ... And although we didn't play as well as we wanted to on offense, I felt like we beat a very good football team, and we're excited about being 1–0."

Rodgers played well the next week at Detroit as well, helping the Packers rally for a 48–25 win. Green Bay trailed, 25–24, midway through the fourth quarter before scoring the final 24 points of the game. Rodgers was sharp again, completing 24-of-38 for 328 yards and three TDs. Rodgers' first road start also produced his first fourth-quarter comeback, and he became the first Green Bay quarterback to start his career 2–0 since Scott Hunter in 1971.

"I thought Aaron put together a fine performance," McCarthy said. "There are a couple of things he can learn from. I thought he did a really good job of using his feet to stay out of bad situations; very decisive with the ball. I thought he threw the ball very well today. I thought he had a real nice day today."

Rodgers threw all three of his TD passes in the first 24 minutes of the game as the Packers raced to a 21–0 lead. Then, after the Lions had rallied back to take a one-point lead, Rodgers hit Jennings with a 60-yard pass to set up the go-ahead field goal. Green Bay never trailed again.

"My idol growing up, Joe Montana, was a guy who could always bring his team back in the fourth quarter; a guy who his teammates trusted with the ball in his hands late in the game," Rodgers said. "You don't want to have a lot of comebacks because you want to be ahead in the game, but unfortunately our lead dwindled. Detroit got the crowd back in the game, and we were able to put together really one big play, Greg Jennings with a big catch and run, and then a big field goal by Mason (Crosby)."

Aaron Rodgers (left) celebrates with injured teammate Ruvell Martin after throwing a touchdown pass against the Detroit Lions in Week 2, 2008.

The Packers were 2-0, sitting atop the NFC North, and looking pretty good for staying with Rodgers instead Favre. Over the next few weeks, that would all change. Green Bay's slide started with a 27–16 home loss to Dallas. Ironically, Rodgers' play against those same Cowboys 10 months earlier was a big reason the Packers' brass felt confident cutting the cord with Favre.

Rodgers didn't do anything to submarine Green Bay's chances of defeating the Cowboys. But he wasn't special, either. Rodgers finished the night 22-of-39 for 290 yards with no touchdowns and no interceptions. However, 146 of Rodgers' passing yards came in the fourth quarter when the contest had been decided.

"You've got to give Dallas credit," Rodgers said afterward. "I didn't have a lot of lanes tonight, didn't throw the ball as well as I wanted to, and they did a nice job with their pass rush." For Rodgers, it was a major difference from the first two weeks of the year in which he'd made Packer Nation stop clamoring for Favre— at least temporarily.

In Green Bay's wins over Minnesota and Detroit, Rodgers had posted a lights-out passer rating of 117.8. He had completed 70.0 percent of his throws with four touchdowns and no interceptions. Rodgers never could get the offense on track against Dallas, though. Rodgers was too slow with his progressions and took five sacks, the most a Green Bay quarterback had taken since Sept. 17, 2000. The Packers were just 1-for-3 in the red zone and converted only 4-of-14 third downs (28.6 percent).

"We wanted to get him uncomfortable and make him run around a little bit," Dallas defensive end Marcus Spears said. "He was able to scramble against other teams, so our rush lanes were very important. We also wanted to get our hands up and cover receivers downfield. Overall, we did a pretty good job."

Unfortunately for Rodgers and the Packers, this was just the start of an ugly skid. The next week, Rodgers threw three interceptions, had a passer rating of just 55.9, and the Packers fell in Tampa Bay, 30–21. Of greater concern, though, was the fact that Rodgers suffered a sprained throwing shoulder and couldn't finish the game.

Throughout the following week, Rodgers' status for Green Bay's Week 5

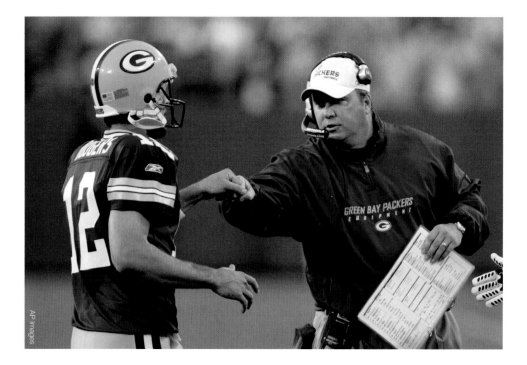

home game with Atlanta was up in the air. "My understanding is the strength is definitely improving, and I'm sure there's going to be some pain as he works through the progress of the evaluation," McCarthy said two days before the Falcons' game. "Frankly, you hand in the inactives at 10:30 [AM], and I'm sure we'll make our decision close to then."

By that time, Rodgers had shown enough improvement to start against the Falcons. Rodgers had a big day, too, throwing for 313 yards, three TDs, and posting a 109.4 passer rating. But with the Packers trailing, 20–17 midway through the fourth quarter and trying to rally,

Rodgers was intercepted by Atlanta's Michael Boley. The Falcons scored three plays later and held on for a 27–24 win.

Green Bay had fallen to 2–3, the same number of losses it suffered in all of 2007. The Packers' losing streak was now three games, and the toughest part of their schedule was looming. "You don't push the panic button," Packers cornerback Tramon Williams said. "All you can do is go back to the drawing board and clean up mistakes you've been making. The problem is they aren't new mistakes. They're the same mistakes we've been making all year long, and we still haven't fixed them. I guess that's troubling."

Packers head coach Mike McCarthy, part of the San Francisco 49ers staff that passed on drafting Aaron Rodgers, was thrilled to have him in Green Bay.

Green Bay solved some of those problems the following week with a 27–17 win at Seattle. Rodgers then notched his biggest NFL win, a 34–14 victory over Peyton Manning and Indianapolis. "Peyton's a great quarterback," Rodgers said. "He's established. He's been to a number of Pro Bowls. He's won a Super Bowl, he's won MVPs. I hope one day to be able to be mentioned in the same sentence more than just when we play them. But I haven't proven anything that he's proven yet."

On this night, though, Rodgers got the better of Manning. Rodgers was an extremely steady 21-of-28 for 186 yards and one TD pass. Manning, on the other hand, completed just 21-of-42 passes and was intercepted twice.

Now, heading into the bye week, the Packers had new life. Green Bay was 4–3, had a two-game winning streak, and was tied atop the NFC North with Chicago. "I think it's just a big confidence boost for our team," Rodgers said. "We were 3–3 coming into this one and … felt like we needed this going into the bye week."

The bye week turned out to be an eventful period for Rodgers. During that two-week stretch, negotiations heated up for a contract extension, and Rodgers eventually signed a six-year, $66 million extension. "As we talked about in the past, we try to be proactive in our discussions with our current players, and we felt like this was an appropriate time to try to come to an agreement with Aaron," Packers general manager Ted Thompson said. "We feel like this is good for the organization and the players, and we will continue this approach as we move forward."

At the time, Rodgers had made just seven career starts. But the Packers believed in what they saw, and Rodgers believed in the Packers. "It means a lot," Rodgers said of signing the long-term deal. "I'm very excited knowing that my future is going to be here in Green Bay."

The immediate future, though, became an exercise in frustration. First, the Packers fell in overtime to undefeated Tennessee, 19–16. Then Green Bay dropped a 28–27 decision at Minnesota when Mason Crosby narrowly missed a 52-yard field goal in the closing seconds.

Those losses left the Packers 0–3 in games decided by four points or fewer.

And at 4–5, Green Bay's season was hanging by a thread. "The critical situations that we haven't been able to overcome, it's the National Football League," McCarthy said. "You can break it down to explosive gains, negative plays, the different things that go on, and the factor hasn't fallen on our side. We have to continue to work, continue to make those critical plays at critical times, and we haven't done that. We have five losses, and you can point to specific plays in every single one of those games. We need to turn some of those around in our favor."

The Packers showed signs of life the following week with a 37–3 dismantling of Chicago. Rodgers led the charge, completing 23-of-30 passes for 227 yards and two TDs. Now, with six games remaining, the Packers, Bears, and Vikings were all tied for the division lead with 5–5 records.

"It's going to be very exciting for all of us," Rodgers said after the game. "We feel like we're going to have to win every game. We control our own destiny now because I know we have the tie-breaker over Chicago, and we have the division tie-breaker over Minnesota. So we couldn't ask for a better position. It's been an up-and-down season, but we played the way we feel we're capable of playing [against Chicago], and we're very confident."

That confidence was shattered, though, over the next month. Remarkably, Green Bay lost five straight games—its longest slide since 1990—and completely fell out of the playoff picture. The Packers were routed by New Orleans, 51–29, on a Monday night. But Green Bay's next four losses were by a combined 14 points, and it had chances to win each game. In a 35–31 home loss to Carolina, Rodgers was white hot much of the day, throwing for 298 yards and three TDs. But with a chance to rally his team late, Rodgers badly underthrew Donald Driver, and Panthers middle linebacker Jon Beason intercepted.

"To be honest with you, I'm getting kind of tired of learning from experiences like this," said Rodgers, whose team fell to 5–7 after the loss. "It's pretty frustrating when you lose games like that. You've got to be critical of yourself. I feel like I competed today, but I didn't throw the ball as well as I wanted to at times. As a quarterback, you want the ball in your hands under two minutes with a chance to lead your team to victory."

One week later, Texans' kicker Kris Brown drilled a 40-yard field goal on the final play of the game to lift Houston to a 24–21 win. "It's disappointing," Rodgers said. "We had a chance to win. It's kind of gone the same script. We start slow, wait for somebody to make a play. Somebody does, then we start turning it on the offensive side of the ball, get the ball in good position, have an opportunity to win the game, and we don't. So that's probably the most frustrating part."

A 20–16 road loss in Jacksonville followed. The Packers then slid all the way to 5–10 after a 20–17 loss in Chicago. Through it all, Rodgers was putting up big numbers. He just wasn't delivering at crunch time, and the Packers couldn't buy a win if the game was close.

"We've just come up short so many times this year," Rodgers said. "We're not going to make excuses. We've had the opportunity in just about every one of those games. You look at the games we've lost; we've lost with opportunities to win in the last minutes. Make a play and win in the last minutes. We haven't done that."

Green Bay finished the season with a 31–21 win over Detroit, which made the Lions the NFL's first winless team since Tampa Bay in 1976. Rodgers and Driver hooked up on a 71-yard TD to ice the game and ensure the Packers wouldn't fall victim to the hapless Lions.

Still Green Bay's season had been a giant disappointment. In a matter of 11 months, the Packers had gone from playing in an NFC Championship Game to posting a 6–10 record and finishing in third place in a watered-down NFC North. "We didn't want to lose, no. No we didn't," Rodgers said. "But really it's not on your mind once the game starts. We ourselves, we were on a five-game losing streak, so we needed this one to get some momentum going into the next season."

Afterward, Rodgers was conducting his final press conference of 2008 and had answered 21 questions. That, of course, was nothing compared to the thousands he'd fielded during an exhausting season.

Aaron Rodgers' ability to escape the pocket and beat defenses with his legs was a dimension of the quarterback position the Packers hadn't enjoyed for years.

As the question-and-answer session was coming to a close, Adam Woullard, a gifted member of the Packers public relations staff, said, "Last one please." Rodgers chimed in, "Make it a good one." Remarkably, no one had anything left. It may have been the first time all season that Rodgers could exhale.

Rodgers' first year as the starter in Green Bay was now behind him, and the Packers' 6–10 record would eat at him throughout the entire offseason. But Rodgers had played well, and Green Bay's future at the position appeared bright. Rodgers threw for 4,038 yards, 28 touchdowns, and just 13 interceptions in that 2008 campaign. He completed 63.6 percent of his passes, and his passer rating was an impressive 93.8.

"I played well in stretches, and I didn't play well at times," Rodgers said. "I think I was a little bit too inconsistent at times, and I'm going to be back to work. I'm going to come back when we start and go through another quarterback school and try to get ready to have an even better year next year."

While the move from Favre to Rodgers was painful, awkward, and extremely drawn out, no one inside Green Bay's organization was looking back. "I think we definitely made the right move at the quarterback position," McCarthy said of the switch to Rodgers. "I was pleased with the productivity from the quarterback position. From an individual standpoint, I think Aaron Rodgers played at a very steady, steady level, which was a high level based on his statistics. He has given us a baseline, a standard that we will hold him to and the offensive group as we move forward."

Rodgers' success was even more impressive considering he was trying to fill the shoes of arguably the greatest player in Packer history. And with Favre still playing for the New York Jets, his shadow loomed incredibly large all season. But Rodgers handled the circus-like atmosphere throughout training camp with class. Then he played at a relatively high level all season.

"I think the thing that impressed me the most about Aaron was how well he handled himself," Packers No. 2 quarterback Matt Flynn said. "He said all the right things. He did all the right things, and I think he became the leader of this team, for sure."

What Rodgers failed to do was succeed in the clutch. Rodgers had a chance to produce game-winning drives in the final minutes on eight occasions: Tampa Bay, Atlanta, Tennessee, at Minnesota, Carolina, Houston, Jacksonville, and at Chicago. Rodgers failed all eight times, and in games decided by four points or fewer , the Packers went 0–7.

As Rodgers left Green Bay that December for a trip in Australia, he knew his No. 1 area for growth was late-game situations. "Yeah, that's the NFL right there," Rodgers said. "Games are won and lost by two or three plays just about every game. We've got to make those plays next year. There's going to be similar situations, we're going to have a lot of our guys back, and we're going to need to win those close games."

Still, the good outweighed the bad with Rodgers. Rodgers' accuracy and arm strength were both better than advertised. His decision-making and command of the offense were impressive. In addition, he fought through a sprained right-shoulder injury and started all 16 games.

That's why the Packers felt awfully good about the quarterbacking situation.

"He held true to the type of quarterback that I felt he was going to be as far as his decision-making ability and his ball accuracy," McCarthy said. "That's something that he showed in his opportunities as a young player in our first couple of years here, and he was able to sustain that for 16 games. That's what I was most pleased about.

"There are a number of things he was very positive (in). I thought he was very good outside of the pocket making plays with his feet. I thought he was smart in space. He took a couple of hits earlier in the season that you didn't see later in the season. The beauty of Aaron is he is young, and he has the opportunity to only improve. But I think he has a good baseline to start from."

Indeed he did. And Rodgers was only getting started. ■

CHAPTER 7

2009: MOVING TOWARD THE TOP

As 2009 dawned, there was renewed hope and optimism in the NFL's smallest city. From a team standpoint, the 2008 campaign had been one of the most disappointing in franchise history. In fact, Green Bay's seven-game slide was the longest single-season skid in team history. Mentally, the year had been even more cumbersome. The Favre-saga dragged deeper into the summer than necessary, and it was a distraction the Packers couldn't overcome.

One positive, though, was the progress Rodgers showed. Rodgers was far from perfect during that 6–10 campaign, but he entered the season just 25 years old and proved he was capable of handling the position for years to come.

"I just think Aaron Rodgers today has more credibility with his teammates and probably with the media and the fan base," McCarthy said. "I don't think anybody ever questioned whether Aaron Rodgers could be a top-flight quarterback if you watched him practice every day, and that's always the biggest hurdle you have to overcome as any player, particularly at the quarterback position. Can you transfer that to the playing field, and I think that's something that Aaron can really draw from his experience this past year is how consistent that he was as a first-year starter."

Many Packers also seemed genuinely excited after McCarthy overhauled his coaching staff. When the 2008 season ended, McCarthy fired two of his four coordinators, nudged a third one into retirement, and dumped five other assistant coaches. The biggest coaching addition that offseason was defensive coordinator Dom Capers, who had twice been a head coach in the league and led the Carolina Panthers

Aaron Rodgers was still in need of a signature win when the 2009 season started. He got it in the opener, rallying the Packers past arch-rival Chicago.

"THE ONE THING ABOUT OUR BUSINESS, YOU ARE EITHER IMPROVING OR YOU ARE GOING THE OTHER WAY. —Mike McCarthy

to the 1996 NFC Championship Game.

The Packers then selected linebacker Clay Matthews and nose tackle B.J. Raji in what turned out to be a draft for the ages. "The one thing about our business, you are either improving or you are going the other way," McCarthy said. "I'm very excited about the additions."

Green Bay was sharp on the field that summer, too, winning its first three preseason games. Perhaps the greatest chaos came in mid-August, when Favre came out of retirement—again—and signed with divisional foe Minnesota. Twelve months earlier, that type of news would have likely thrown Rodgers off his game. But just days after the announcement, Rodgers lit up the Buffalo Bills and posted a 151.6 passer rating during an easy Packers' preseason win.

"He's got a year under his belt; I think he feels more comfortable every day,"

Packers running back Ryan Grant said of Rodgers. "I think if you ask him, he's on the same page with all the guys. That's been big for us."

Rodgers was extremely big that entire summer and finished with a passer rating of 147.9. He was quick with his reads, dead-on with his accuracy, and commanding in the huddle. "He's in sync right now," McCarthy said. "You have to keep working every day to keep that, but he's had a good preseason." The regular-season opener against Chicago was just days away. And Rodgers and the Packers couldn't wait.

It had been a quiet summer, a productive summer. Rodgers and the offense had sizzled. Capers' defense had been greatly improved. And the Packers were anxious to show their 2008 season was an aberration, not the norm. "I'm not a predictor," Packers general manager Ted

Aaron Rodgers launched his 2009 campaign after another terrific preseason, finishing with a lights-out 147.9 passer rating in the exhibition games.

Thompson said. "I don't do that. I don't want to put up any bulletin-board stuff. I do think this is a good group of guys, and I think it's a good team, and if we play well I think we'll have a chance to win. What that means I don't know.

"Every year is a new year. I do think, especially our first group, has played very well in the preseason. That is preseason, but there is a confident air in our locker room, and I think our guys think that we can hold our own against most people."

Lovie Smith, Jay Cutler, Brian Urlacher, and the Chicago Bears were first up in 2009. The Packers were about to discover exactly what they had.

. . . .

As the 2009 season kicked off, there was one area that bothered Rodgers more than any other: close games. During Rodgers' first season as a starter, the Packers went 0–7 in games decided by four points or less. And eight different times, Rodgers had a chance to pull out a game in the final five minutes and failed each time. "That bothers me a lot," Rodgers said shortly before the season began. "I want to fix that."

One game into the 2009 campaign,

Rodgers was well on his way to repairing it. During Green Bay's season-opener with Chicago, Rodgers came up huge late in a game for the first time in his Packers career. Rodgers hit wideout Greg Jennings with a 50-yard touchdown pass with 1:11 left to lift Green Bay past Chicago, 21–15.

"I don't think I ever lost confidence in myself or my abilities [in 2008], but when you have some struggles and you make some throws you want back late in games, it's good to start a season out and be in a situation where you're called upon and expected to perform late in the game," Rodgers said afterward. "To be able to, in crunch time when it was needed, to come up with a big throw and get [the ball to] our playmaker Greg [Jennings] was very important for myself and also for our team."

Rodgers and Green Bay's offense never could get going against a fired-up Bears defense that night. But years from now, all anyone will remember from this thriller was that Rodgers stepped up with arguably his biggest moment as a Packer. When Rodgers stepped on the field with 2:35 left, his confidence couldn't have been particularly high. The Packers trailed the Bears, 15–13. Green Bay had just 156

yards of total offense and only three points in the second half.

Green Bay began at its own 28-yard line, and four plays later, it faced a third-and-1 from midfield. McCarthy called for a Ryan Grant running play, but when Jennings lined up in the wrong spot, the Packers had to call timeout. "It was my fault," Jennings said. "I actually designed that, to line up on the wrong side of the field so that we could go for the gold. And it got it done for us."

After the timeout, the Bears were expecting run and brought an eighth man into the box with safety Al Afalava. Rodgers ran play-action, and his first option was to tight end Donald Lee on a wheel route. Rodgers first looked right to Lee, which held safety Kevin Payne in place. Jennings, who lined up on the far left, raced past cornerback Nathan Vasher.

Rodgers, who was sacked four times and hit nine others, had terrific protection on this play and lofted a perfect pass. Jennings caught it in stride at the 14 and waltzed in with the game-winner. "I just told the guys, 'Hey, just give me one drive,'" Rodgers said of the game-winning march. "Up front, I went to the linemen and said, 'Hey, let's just protect this one drive. Give me some time, and we're going to go down and score.'"

While that provided a terrific start to the season, the first quarter of the year proved choppy. Green Bay dropped two of its next three games, including a 30–23 loss at Minnesota on *Monday Night Football*. That was the first meeting between Favre and Rodgers, and on that night, Favre got the best of his former understudy. Favre also got revenge on Packers general manager Ted Thompson, the man who chose Rodgers over Favre in the summer of 2007. "I just did what I was expected to do today," Favre said afterward.

And how. Favre orchestrated four drives that went deep into Green Bay territory. And on all four, Favre's Vikings left with touchdowns. Rodgers and the Packers weren't nearly as successful. On three different occasions, Rodgers led the Packers into scoring range. Rodgers fumbled once, threw an interception, and the Packers were also stopped on downs. Three trips. Zero points.

"To have three possessions where you are in their territory and come away with zero points ... two of them were directly

related to mistakes by myself, it's disappointing," Rodgers said. Rodgers finished the night with a career-high 384 yards, a pair of touchdowns, and had a passer rating of 110.6. On paper, those statistics were comparable to Favre's (271 yards, 3 TDs, 135.3 passer rating).

The difference, though, was that Favre and the Vikings made the most of their chances, while Rodgers and the Packers couldn't. "You can't have it," McCarthy said of the turnovers. "They took points off the board."

Green Bay bounced back with consecutive wins over NFL doormats Detroit and Cleveland by a combined score of 57–3 and improved to 4–2. But really, that was simply window dressing for the Packers' November 1 game vs. Minnesota. Brett Favre was coming back to Lambeau Field. Arguably the largest regular-season game in franchise history was just around the corner.

The Packers were trying to treat Favre's return like it was just another game. Same routine. Same preparation. Same everything. Weeks later, many admitted they were simply fooling themselves. "We were so tight for that game … and really the whole time leading up to it,"

Packers defensive end Cullen Jenkins said. "That whole week before Brett came back was really tense."

It showed. During the summer of discontent in 2008, Favre said he wanted to "stick it" to Packers general manager Ted Thompson. In his return to Lambeau Field—the place he'd given Green Bay fans 16 years' worth of mostly terrific memories—Favre did exactly that.

Favre was surgeon-like, carving up Green Bay's secondary with remarkable precision and accuracy and leading the Vikings to a critical 38–26 win. Favre threw four touchdown passes for the 21st time in his career, which tied him with Dan Marino for the most in NFL history, and posted a lights-out passer rating of 128.6.

"Am I pleased with the way these two games have turned out? Absolutely," Favre said of defeating Green Bay twice. "It had nothing to do with trying to prove myself to anyone. I still have a passion for it. It's a little bit tougher to get up and bounce back, but my arm feels great. My mind is in a good place, the team has welcomed me in, and really all the other stuff doesn't matter. I know it makes for a good story. But I'm glad it's over, I'm glad we won both, but I'm not going to sit here

Brett Favre and his Vikings got the better of Aaron Rodgers and the Packers in their first meeting. Minnesota prevailed 30–23 in a Monday night contest at the Metrodome.

> # "I HATE LOSING TO WHOEVER'S AT QUARTERBACK FOR THEM. I HATE LOSING TO THE VIKINGS ESPECIALLY. (THEY'RE) DIVISION RIVALS (AND WE) DON'T LIKE THOSE (LOSSES) AT HOME. —Aaron Rodgers

and throw any daggers."

In Favre's first two games against Green Bay, he went 41-of-59 for 515 yards, threw seven touchdowns, had no interceptions, and finished with a passer rating of 135.9. Most importantly, Minnesota improved to 7–1 and swept the season series against the Packers (4–3).

"We talked a little bit about not doing too much," Vikings coach Brad Childress said. "You have a tendency to do too much sometimes, and I thought he did just about what he needed to do. He didn't get too creative or try to rig anything up. I just thought he kept it in body, didn't get out of body."

In the Packers' locker room, things were much more bleak. Green Bay's hopes at an NFC North title had taken a serious hit. The Packers had struggled for the second time in four weeks against an elite team. And Green Bay's confidence had undoubtedly taken a blow. "I hate losing to whoever's at quarterback for them," Rodgers said. "I hate losing to the Vikings, especially. [They're] division rivals [and we] don't like those [losses] at home."

Rodgers had a rough first half, going 5-of-11 for 38 yards with a 54.4 passer rating. Overall, Green Bay managed just 47 net yards in the half, its fewest since a 31–10 loss in Denver on October 17, 1999. Not surprisingly, the Packers were in a 17–3 hole to the Vikings. "We weren't in a rhythm," Rodgers said of Green Bay's first-half struggles. "I think that's the first thing. That was due to a lack of execution."

Rodgers and the Packers did get rolling

after halftime. In fact, Green Bay scored on four straight possessions—three touchdowns and one field goal—to close to within 31–26. The Packers abandoned their putrid rushing game and let Rodgers wing it around against Minnesota's overmatched secondary. And Rodgers had a second-half passer rating of 128.3 after completing 21 of 30 attempts for 249 yards, three touchdowns, and no interceptions.

"I started hitting guys that were open," Rodgers said. "The first half I struggled, missed a couple throws I should have hit. When we get into a rhythm on offense, we're tough to stop." Trailing 31–26 with 8:13 left, Rodgers and the Packers took over at their own 19. Just two plays later, the Packers had marched to Minnesota's 28. But on second-and-3, Rodgers took his sixth sack of the game, losing five yards on the play. Rodgers then threw incomplete on third down, and Mason Crosby proceeded to miss a 51-yard field goal.

Brett Favre and the Vikings reclaimed the ball—and quickly regained all momentum. On Minnesota's first play, Favre hit Adrian Peterson for 44 yards on a screen pass. Then two plays later, Favre

hummed a 16-yard TD pass to Bernard Berrian. Ball game.

Again, doubts about Rodgers' ability to deliver in the clutch persisted. "You look at everything that evolves around your football team, and Aaron is part of the solution," Packers coach Mike McCarthy said. "There is no doubt about it. He is definitely one of the positives, but he has things he needs to work on too, just like every member of our football team."

The Packers figured to get well the following week with a trip to Tampa Bay to face the 0–7 Buccaneers. Green Bay entered the game as a 10-point favorite, but they played arguably their worst game of the McCarthy era and fell to hapless Tampa Bay, 38–28.

"I've been asked about the rebound from Minnesota; hell, we have to rebound from Tampa Bay," McCarthy said. "We've had two tough losses in a row here, and we need to handle the adversity that's in front of us. We didn't handle the adversity of the way the game went up and down as a team, and that starts with me."

The adversity on the field was nothing, though, compared to the difficulties off of it. One day after the brutal loss, the

Packers' offense gathered to clear the air—and clear the air they did. "There were some deep-seated emotions in that room that needed to get out—that guys were holding in," Rodgers said. "It was great. There were a lot of harsh words said, but at the end of the day, we moved on together.

"A lot of times when there is strife on a team it can get out in the wrong way—guys talking in the media on their own or behind the scenes—but we sat in the room as an offense and said, 'What are the main issues here?' Myself, Donald (Driver), and different guys spoke up, and we got our issues on the table and moved forward as a team. It wasn't a divided locker room. We stayed together, talked about our problems, and moved forward together."

The Packers were moving forward with a disappointing 4–4 record. With a brutal second-half schedule still looming, much of Packer Nation was wondering if 2009 would be another lost year.

....

The following week, Dallas came to Lambeau Field winners of four straight and leading the NFC East with a 6–2 mark. Green Bay's season, meanwhile, was hanging by a string. The Packers entered as a 3-point underdog on their own field, knowing another loss might keep them from the postseason. "The importance and urgency has to increase," McCarthy said.

To the surprise of many, it did. Rodgers keyed a pair of huge fourth-quarter touchdown drives, running for one score and throwing for another. Green Bay held Dallas to season lows in rushing yards (61) and total yards (278). And the Packers exited with a critical 17–7 victory.

"It was a big win for us definitely," Rodgers said afterward. "We knew (being) 4–4 (and) playing a very good team, it was an important time in our season to get back in this race. I think a lot of people were thinking this was going to be the end of the road for us and going to be a turning point for the negative for us this season. But it was a big win for our team."

It sure was. Since the start of the 2008 season, Green Bay had been 10–14 and had defeated only two teams with winning records. But this was arguably Green Bay's most impressive win under Rodgers. "We said all week, if we want this season to turn out the way we think it should, we have to make a run, and it needs to start this week," fullback John Kuhn said. "It can't start next week, it

Rodgers was unable to rally the Packers from a big deficit against visiting Minnesota during their second 2009 meeting. Like the earlier game, Favre and the Vikings prevailed, this time 38–26.

"I WOULD CLEARLY SAY THAT AARON RODGERS HAS FALLEN INTO THE CLASSIFICATION OF A FRANCHISE QUARTERBACK.

—Mike McCarthy

can't start on Thanksgiving [against Detroit], and it can't start in December. It has to start now. This is just a starting point, though. It isn't anything special. We're going to enjoy the win for a day or two, then get right back at it."

Boy, did they ever. The Dallas game started a five-game winning streak that saw Green Bay climb to 9–4, jump right back into the playoff hunt, and silence many that doubted Rodgers and the Packers. "There are a lot of positive aspects and variables of our football team," McCarthy said. "The most important thing is those positive things, we need them to show up every week, and we need to continue to improve."

The Packers—and Rodgers—were both riding high. Green Bay followed its win over Dallas with a 30–24 win over San Francisco. Rodgers was extremely sharp that day, going 32-of-45 with two TD passes—

including a 64-yarder to Greg Jennings.

The Packers then drilled Detroit, 34–12, on Thanksgiving. Rodgers again had a huge day with three TD passes, 348 passing yards, and no interceptions. "Consistent," McCarthy said of Rodgers. "He's doing a very good job of running the offense, not taking chances. I think the pass protection has improved week to week, and he's just doing a great job of running the offense. We've been playing at a high level here on offense."

That didn't change the following week against a terrific Baltimore defense. Rodgers threw three touchdowns—including two to standout tight end Jermichael Finley—and the Packers upended the Ravens, 27–14.

The following week, Green Bay ventured south to face archrival Chicago. The Bears had lost four of five and were 5–7 overall and virtually eliminated from postseason play. But nothing is ever easy when these teams meet, and it wasn't on this day either.

The Packers trailed, 14–13, in the fourth quarter when Nick Collins intercepted Chicago's Jay Cutler and returned the pick to the Bears' 11-yard line. Two plays later, Ryan Grant banged in, and the Packers eventually escaped with a 21–14 win. The Packers were now 9–4, and their five-game winning streak was their third-longest of the decade. Capers' defense was improving by the week. Rodgers had the offense humming along.

There were still three games remaining. But Rodgers had certainly won over his head coach. "I would clearly say that Aaron Rodgers has fallen into the classification of a franchise quarterback," McCarthy said. "He has played at that level. I know it's only been a year and a half or a year and three-quarters. I think he's definitely at that level of play, so I just think that in itself tells you how we feel about him and his value to our football team."

The following week, the Packers saw a quarterback just as deadly: Pittsburgh's Ben Roethlisberger. Little did anyone know, but it was a prelude of things to come. On a cold December day in Pittsburgh, Rodgers and Roethlisberger engaged in classic shootout.

Rodgers was brilliant throughout, throwing for 383 yards, three touchdowns, and rushing for a fourth score. In fact, Rodgers was so deadly that after the Steelers took a 30–28 lead with four minutes left, Pittsburgh coach Mike Tomlin made the unusual decision to try an onside kick. "In the latter part of the fourth quarter, I felt that both offenses were capable of moving the football," Tomlin said. "We had 30 minutes of evidence to show they could also drive the ball on us. That's why we took the risk when we did."

It didn't pay off, as Pittsburgh's onside kick went just nine yards. Then Rodgers hit James Jones with a 24-yard TD pass with 2:06 remaining to put the Packers back ahead, 36–30. Pittsburgh still had two minutes left, though, which was a lifetime in this thriller. And on the final play of the game, Roethlisberger hit Mike Wallace in the left corner of the end zone for a 19-yard TD and a 37–36 Steelers win.

"You lose on a last-second play, with a spectacular throw and catch, it's tough,"

"WE'RE DOING A LOT OF GOOD THINGS RIGHT NOW, AND WE WANT TO BE SURE NOT TO TAKE OUR FOOT OFF THE GAS.

—Daryn Colledge

Packers linebacker Clay Matthews said. "Hindsight's always 20-20, but we knew what we were getting ourselves into. It was a dogfight." Roethlisberger finished with a remarkable 503 passing yards, the most ever by a Pittsburgh quarterback. The five-game winning streak was over. And the Packers still had some work to do to earn a playoff spot.

But the fact that Green Bay had gone to Pittsburgh and played the defending Super Bowl champs toe-to-toe was highly encouraging. "We came up one play short, and it will be corrected tomorrow," McCarthy said afterward. "I'm sure there will be a number of opportunities where we could've probably made one play. I think this is classic December football. It came down to the last play of the game, and we didn't get it done."

But one week later, Rodgers and the Packers picked up right where they'd left off. Green Bay rolled up 417 yards of total offense and routed visiting Seattle, 48–10. When Carolina defeated the New York Giants that day, the Packers had clinched their first playoff berth since Favre left. And afterward, several players took a lap around Lambeau Field to acknowledge the fans.

Green Bay followed that with a 33–7 beatdown of host Arizona and finished the regular season 11–5. The Cardinals took a cautious approach to the game and rested many of their key players, knowing they were likely to face Green Bay in the first round of the playoffs. The Packers, meanwhile, tried to add to the momentum they'd established in the second half of the season—something they accomplished with relative ease.

"It's an impressive body of work, the

As the 2009 postseason arrived, Aaron Rodgers and the Packers were red hot, with wins in seven of their last eight games.

waiting on calls to win football games, you're in a mode of excuses," McCarthy said. "The way the game ended, you don't want it to come down to an officiating call. Nobody wants that. You want it to be about player productivity. There was a lot of productivity in that football game, especially from an offensive standpoint. But I'm not going to sit here and try to discredit Arizona's victory by no means, because it really doesn't do any good."

Despite the disappointing end, there was plenty of good for Rodgers and the Packers in 2009. And in many ways, it set the Packers up for much of their 2010 success. Rodgers had a breakout year, finishing fourth in the NFL in passer rating (103.2), passing yards (4,434), and touchdowns (30). He also threw just seven interceptions, and his interception percentage of 1.3 ranked first in football.

Rodgers also became the first quarterback in league history to eclipse more than 4,000 passing yards in each of his first two years as a starter. And Rodgers' 4,434 passing yards were second in team history, behind only Lynn Dickey's 4,458 in 1983. More importantly, though, Green Bay won 11 games after winning just six the previous campaign.

"I think Aaron has had a very good year," McCarthy said of Rodgers. "I don't think there's [any] doubt about that. When you go win it all, I think that's when you start talking about great seasons. But he was definitely a very bright positive for our football team, both on the field and in the locker room, and we feel very good about that as an organization. I definitely felt that he had a very, very good year."

Rodgers didn't throw an interception in 12 of his 16 games, breaking the old mark of 11 held by Bart Starr in 1964. Rodgers also punished defenses with his feet. His 316 rushing yards were the second-most in football by a quarterback. He also scored five rushing touchdowns, the most by a Packer quarterback since Don Majkowski also had five in 1989.

In addition, third down was also a magical one for Rodgers. On that down alone, Rodgers had a 133.5 passer rating, threw 14 TDs, and had no interceptions. Rodgers' 1,710 passing yards on third down were also the most since the stat was originated in 1991. "Aaron Rodgers is a Pro Bowl quarterback, and that's the facts," McCarthy said. "Trust me, I fully

Aaron Rodger is hit in overtime by Cardinals cornerback Michael Adams, causing a fumble that Arizona recovered and returned for the winning touchdown in the NFC Wild Card Game.

understand the greatness of Brett Favre, and I had the opportunity to be part of his career, and he deserves everything that comes his way.

"But this is the beginning of potentially another great career at quarterback here in Green Bay, and [fans] should embrace it. That would be my suggestion if there is any doubt. He's putting up Pro Bowl numbers in both of his seasons. It does come down to winning, winning is important, but he's put together two quality seasons so far."

Rodgers also appeared to turn a corner sometime around the Dallas game. He started making quicker decisions, and instead of typically playing things safe, he tried making plays each week that only the NFL's elite are capable of. Rodgers was sacked 37 times in the first eight games of the year, with many of those being his fault. But Rodgers showed dramatic improvement in the second half of the year when he was sacked just 13 times in the final eight games.

"I'm very impressed," Packers cornerback Charles Woodson said of Rodgers. "The numbers speak for themselves, to go back-to-back seasons with 4,000 yards. I don't know too many quarterbacks that have gone through the transition that he had to go through when Brett left the team.

"For him to go through that this year, to go through the numerous amount of sacks that he has gone through, and taking a lot of heat for supposedly holding the football too long, and that sort of thing. He comes to work every day, prepares every day like a winning quarterback, and then on Sundays he shows up. Again, he keeps getting up off the ground and making plays for this team. There is not enough that can be said about what he has done this year."

Of course, the disappointing conclusion would linger with Green Bay's players throughout a long offseason. And when 2010 rolled around, the Packers insisted they'd be hungrier than ever. "This is just going to make myself and these guys want it that much more," Rodgers said of the loss to Arizona. "It might not look like we came that close, but we still feel like we were close to achieving all the goals we set forth at the beginning of the season." Indeed they were.

Little did anyone know it, but 12 months later those goals would be met. ∎

Despite his phenomenal second-half performance against the Cardinals, Rodgers' second season as starter ended in frustration when the Packers fell in the first round of the playoffs.

CHAPTER 8

2010: REGULAR SEASON ROLLER-COASTER

Bold. Brash. Bombastic. That's how the 2010 Packers were going to operate. When the Packers concluded their offseason program in late June, they lightened the mood by holding a home run hitting contest. Rookie offensive tackle Bryan Bulaga won the event, and for his efforts, was presented a broken-down car. While many chuckled at Bulaga's new vehicle, the message on the car was no laughing matter. On the driver's side, it read: "To Super Bowl—Dallas." "I definitely think we're positioned to do that," veteran wideout Donald Driver said. "Super Bowl's the goal, and I don't think we're going to be shy about saying it."

Later that summer, Rodgers and several of his teammates showed up at the annual Welcome Back Packers Luncheon. They did so wearing cowboy hats and bolo

ties. By all accounts, the stunt was Rodgers' idea. The message was also crystal clear: Green Bay's goal was to finish its season in Arlington, Texas, home of Super Bowl XLV.

"I have every intention and belief that we have the capability of winning the Super Bowl," Packers coach Mike McCarthy said. "Every decision that we make toward our football team, toward our program, toward our environment is always trying to improve our football team."

As the 2010 season dawned, the Packers were everybody's darlings. Several national publications had picked Green Bay to win the Super Bowl, even though it hadn't won a playoff game in the post-Favre era. The Packers, themselves, were doing nothing to quiet the noise. "I just had our team meeting, and

Aaron Rodgers had another terrific preseason in 2010 and became a hot pick for MVP honors.

"I HAVE EVERY INTENTION AND BELIEF THAT WE HAVE THE CAPABILITY OF WINNING THE SUPER BOWL. —Mike McCarthy"

we talked about winning the Super Bowl," McCarthy said the day before training camp began. "We talked about where it is played at and the relevance of our team meeting room.

"The only team pictures that are in that room are the team pictures of the world champions of the Green Bay Packers. Everything that we have done throughout the offseason and everything that we'll do starting tomorrow will be taking a step to being the next team up on that wall. That's our goal."

Rodgers was also a hot pick for MVP honors after another stellar preseason. In three outings that summer, Rodgers threw for six touchdowns, no interceptions, and posted a ridiculous passer rating of 141.2. "It's honestly never entered my thought process," Rodgers said of the MVP talk. "You know, the awards and the predictions and stuff, really, I think that's preseason

fodder. Just stuff to chew on while the games may not be as meaningful. But once we get into the everyday grind of the season, guys are just focused on that week."

As the season began, there were several striking parallels to Green Bay's 1996 team—the last Packers' squad to win a Super Bowl. Rodgers was 26 when the season began, the same age Brett Favre was at the start of 1996. Both players were also beginning their sixth NFL season. Ted Thompson was 57 at the start of the 2010 season and beginning his sixth year as Green Bay's general manager. Back in 1996, Ron Wolf was 57 and beginning his fifth full season as the Packers' GM.

Finally, McCarthy was 46 when the 2010 season opened and starting his fifth year as the Packers' head coach. In 1996, Mike Holmgren, 48, was also beginning his fifth year as the Packers' head coach. "That is crazy," Packers wideout Jordy

Nelson said. "I know you guys can do a lot with stats, but that one is pretty wild."

Not everyone was buying into the hype, though, including some members of Green Bay's last Super Bowl team. The Packers of 1996 were built through a variety of ways: the NFL Draft, free agency, trades, etc. But Thompson never dabbled much in free agency, choosing instead to build his roster almost entirely through the NFL Draft and then develop talent internally. As the season began, many from the old guard wondered exactly how far Thompson could eventually take this franchise.

"You have to make a decision as a general manager: do you want to win championships or do you want to win games?" asked former safety LeRoy Butler, who made four Pro Bowls during his 12-year Packer career. "Ted's going to win games because of Aaron [Rodgers] and because he drafts well. But unless he changes his philosophy when it comes to free agency, it's going to be hard to win championships.

"Right now, the gap between Minnesota and the Packers is huge if Brett [Favre] comes back. How are the Packers going to close that gap? By just drafting a bunch of young guys? The thing is, Ted doesn't believe in getting a 30-year-old veteran to help you do that. He wants to fill his holes with young guys."

When the 1995 Packers had lost in the NFC Championship Game at Dallas, Wolf added free agents such as defensive tackle Santana Dotson, kick returner Desmond Howard, wideout Don Beebe, left tackle Bruce Wilkerson, and linebacker Ron Cox, then also traded for safety Eugene Robinson. Those moves helped get the Packers over the hump the following season.

While the prospects for Green Bay's 2010 season were extremely bright, Thompson had been quiet the entire offseason. And many wondered if his philosophy could ever take the Packers to the promised land. "I know we added some veterans to help us get over the hump," former Packers wideout Robert Brooks said. "But if you've got players who can step in and play, it doesn't matter if they're rookies or if they've been around a long time. Me personally, I'm really excited about this Packers team coming up."

So were the Packers themselves. With

the season-opener in Philadelphia just days away, the Packers were bringing back 21 of 22 preferred starters. Rodgers' combination of physical skills and knowledge of the offense was better than ever. Green Bay's young talent was blossoming. And McCarthy had the total backing of the locker room.

Big things appeared in store. "We talked about the Super Bowl expectations, we set our goals for the season on the first day of training camp," McCarthy said. "I like the confidence of our team, but we're at the starting line." Of what promised to be one remarkable journey.

As the 2010 season opened, Green Bay's star power matched any in football. Jermichael Finley was coming off a season in which his 55 catches were the second-most in team history by a tight end. Finley also finished the year with a memorable 159-yard effort in the playoff loss to Arizona.

The wide receiver quartet of Greg Jennings, Donald Driver, Jordy Nelson, and James Jones matched any in football. Running back Ryan Grant, one of the game's more underappreciated players, had 11 TDs in 2009 and nearly 2,500 rushing yards over the last two seasons.

Defensively, cornerback Charles Woodson was the NFL's reigning MVP. Linebacker Clay Matthews set a franchise rookie record with 10 sacks during his first year, and safety Nick Collins had played in consecutive Pro Bowls.

But with Rodgers beginning his sixth season—and third as the starter—the Packers were officially his team. And like Lambeau, Hutson, Lombardi, Starr, and Favre before him, Rodgers was now the face of the Packers. "It's not something I think about a whole lot," Rodgers said. "I realize my position on this team as quarterback kind of warrants some of that stuff. But as far as a responsibility to that, I am definitely OK with that."

The Packers were certainly okay with it, as well. Green Bay opened the 2010 season at Philadelphia—a team going through a similar transition to what the Packers endured in 2008. The Eagles had parted with veteran quarterback Donovan McNabb that offseason and were turning the reigns over to young Kevin Kolb. The situation mirrored that of Green Bay's move from Favre to Rodgers two years earlier.

"We've definitely conversed more than once in the last few months," Rodgers said of he and Kolb. "He reached out to me and wanted my number. That was a no-brainer for me. I was just honored that he wanted to seek my input-slash-advice.

"I'm definitely a fan of his. Having been in a similar situation, he's definitely a guy I'm pulling for 15 weeks out of the season. He's a very talented guy. I have no doubt he's going to make a very smooth transition."

Well, not quite. Kolb struggled early, then was knocked out of the game after suffering a concussion on a sack from Matthews. Michael Vick came in, was dynamic, and never relinquished the starting job. Despite Vick's best efforts, the Packers were too much for the Eagles.

Green Bay built a 27–10 lead behind two Rodgers' TD passes and a TD run from John Kuhn. The Packers then held on as Vick mounted a furious fourth-quarter rally and won in Philadelphia for the first time since 1962, 27–20. "I thought it was a very gutty performance on both sides of the field, and we feel very fortunate to come out of here with a win," McCarthy said. "This is a tough place to play, and it's a tough football team to play against."

Green Bay didn't leave unscathed,

As the 2010 season began, Aaron Rodgers had won over most of the Green Bay Packers fan base.

Aaron Rodgers accounted for three touchdowns as the Packers routed the Buffalo Bills 34–7 and improved to 2–0.

"WE'RE NOT PLAYING CHAMPIONSHIP FOOTBALL RIGHT NOW.... BUT THERE'S A LOT OF SEASON LEFT. —Donald Lee

though. Grant was lost for the year with an ankle injury, and the Packers would have to move forward without their No. 1 running back. "Ryan Grant is exactly the type of individual you want on your team and in your program, the way he goes about his business," McCarthy said. "He is a hard-working, tough guy, no-nonsense, no-excuse individual, and he is a very good teammate. So the personal angle of Ryan's injury is definitely difficult."

Fortunately for the Packers, NFL doormat Buffalo was up next, and Green Bay was able to ease into life without Grant. Matthews had three more sacks, pushing his NFL-leading total to six. Rodgers threw for 255 yards and accounted for three touchdowns as the Packers rolled to a 34–7 win.

One of the few things that didn't go right came when Rodgers scrambled for a touchdown, but was far from graceful on his Lambeau Leap. "The guys gave me a

hard time on the sideline," Rodgers said. "But I told them, 'Look, I was tired.'"

The Packers hadn't been perfect their first two games. Far from. But they were 2–0 and headed to Chicago for a first-place showdown with the undefeated Bears. Chicago had finished just 7–9 the previous season, but the Bears defense—decimated by injury in 2009—was healthy again and playing at a high level. And quarterback Jay Cutler, now in his second season in Chicago, was maturing.

"I think they are playing with a lot of confidence, very good tempo on defense," McCarthy said of the Bears. "It looks like they have been productive on offense, and their special teams has always been a challenge. We are looking for this to be a heck of a football game on Monday night."

It was. It just wasn't the outcome Green Bay hoped for. The Packers set a new team record with 18 penalties. Chicago's Devin Hester returned a punt 62 yards for a touchdown, his first return for a score in three years. And Packers wideout James Jones had a critical late-game fumble that set up Chicago's Robbie Gould for a chip shot field goal that gave the Bears a 20–17 win. "It was an uncharacteristic game on offense for us, well, just as a team," Rodgers said. "Way too many penalties."

Rodgers was sharp, completing 34 of 45 passes for 316 yards and accounting for two touchdowns. But the penalties, two Green Bay turnovers, and rotten special teams play were too much to overcome. "We'll take a look at the film, but [18] penalties, that doesn't cut it," McCarthy said. "You can't play football like that."

Green Bay wasn't much better the following week, but they held off Detroit for a 28–26 win. The Packers were at the quarter pole in their season and were 3–1 overall. But Green Bay wasn't playing at nearly the same level it had all summer, and that Super Bowl talk had certainly quieted.

"There's a lot of things we've got to clean up and get better at," said linebacker Brady Poppinga. "I don't think anyone's totally happy with how we're playing right now. But we are 3–1. That's a good thing."

Green Bay's special teams, a bugaboo for years, continued to spring leaks. The running game had yet to find its legs without Grant. And the defense allowed 331 passing yards to Lions career backup Shaun Hill. The offense did just enough, though, as Rodgers threw first-half touchdowns to Driver, Finley, and Jennings, and the Packers survived a late Detroit surge.

The biggest drawback, though, was injuries. The Packers lost veteran right tackle Mark Tauscher (shoulder), inside linebacker Nick Barnett (wrist), and rookie safety Morgan Burnett (ACL) in this game, and all three didn't play again in 2010. "We're not playing championship football right now, I'd agree with that," tight end Donald Lee said. "But there's a lot of season left."

Unfortunately for the Packers, their season was about to get worse before it got better. Green Bay played arguably its worst game of the season and dropped a 16–13 overtime decision in Washington the following week. The Redskins overcame a 10-point, fourth-quarter deficit to stun Green Bay.

Injuries continued to mount, as well. Rodgers suffered a concussion in the loss, while both Finley (knee), defensive end Mike Neal (shoulder), and special teams ace Derrick Martin (knee) suffered season-ending injuries. "There is no 'woe is me' here," McCarthy proclaimed after the Redskins loss. "This is the National Football League. It's a dynamic business. Not at the extent of getting players hurt, I like where we are at as a team. I think this is an excellent opportunity for us to show what we are about. I know there is probably doubt outside the room."

That was true, and that doubt got even greater when the Packers dropped a 23–20 overtime decision to Miami and fell to 3–3. The Packers were now just 1–3 in 2010 in games decided by four points or less and 1–11 since Favre departed.

"We've just got to pull through and find a way to win," running back Brandon Jackson said. "I don't know how. We've just got to win. Just got to win. All I know is we have to play better. We have to run better, we have throw better, we have to catch better. We're way better than what the record says, but we are what the record says. We've just got to come out and play better for four quarters and not give an opponent a chance to come back and win the ball game."

Green Bay's defense, which was playing without Matthews, did its job and got

Despite this Rodgers touchdown, Green Bay self-destructed in their first meeting against the Bears, committing a record 18 penalties en route to a 20–17 loss.

a stop to start overtime. But the offense went three-and-out, and then punter Tim Masthay shanked a 37-yarder. Miami then had to move just 26 yards before getting a game-winning field goal.

"We're definitely not where we want to be," linebacker Desmond Bishop said. "At the same time, it's a long season, and we can definitely get it back on track. We're competitors ... and all it takes is a little tightening of some screws here and there, and I think we're going to be hitting on all cylinders and get going."

It had to happen fast. Favre and the Vikings were coming to town, and Green Bay couldn't afford a repeat of 2009 when it lost to Minnesota twice.

Rodgers and the Packers tried to keep things as normal as possible throughout the week, saying that this was just one of 16 games on the schedule. But everyone knew it was much more than that. Beating Favre and the Vikings would definitely be overcoming a mental hurdle for Rodgers and the Packers, especially after Minnesota had recently traded for wideout Randy Moss. It wasn't easy, but Green Bay posted an impressive 28–24 win.

Aaron Rodgers suffered a concussion during a Week 5 loss to Washington. The Packers also lost standout tight end Jermichael Finley for the rest of the season in the game.

The Packers built a 28–17 third-quarter lead and then held on down the stretch. Favre had rallied the Vikings to within 28–24 and drove Minnesota to Green Bay's 20-yard line. But Favre's fourth-down pass to the end zone for Moss was too high, and the Packers notched an enormous win.

"A loss could have been devastating," said Tramon Williams, who was in coverage on Moss on the Vikings' final offensive play. "It would have been another loss to Minnesota. Whew." Whew is right.

It was far too early in the year to call Green Bay's win a "season saver." But there's no doubt a third straight loss would have been extremely damaging on many levels. After losing twice to Minnesota in 2009, many of the Packers admitted there was somewhat of a "hangover" effect. This was the type of narrow win that had avoided Green Bay for much of the Aaron Rodgers—Mike McCarthy era.

Doing it against Favre and the Vikings made it even sweeter. "It was a little more special," Rodgers said. "Because of the significance of where we're at in the season, 3–3 coming in, our opponent, [a] division opponent, our biggest rival, and the close score, the way it ended. It definitely is a special night for us."

In addition, Rodgers got the best of his individual battle with Favre. Rodgers threw for two touchdowns, two interceptions, and had an 84.8 passer rating. Favre struggled and threw three interceptions, one touchdown, and posted just a 50.4 passer rating.

With Chicago starting to struggle, the Packers were again tied atop the NFC North at 4–3, while the Vikings fell to 2–4. And with every team in the NFC having lost at least twice, the conference was once again wide open. "I think these are just the type of games you have to win if you want to be a good team," linebacker A.J. Hawk said.

"We lost a couple games like this in the last couple weeks that we knew we could have had. But that's how it goes. It's a long season. We've just got to keep going. It's not really about anyone else. If we take care of our job, we'll be where we want to be. This is one tiny little step, and we're going to keep moving."

They did. Rodgers and the offense

By the time the 2010 regular season had ended, Aaron Rodgers had defeated Brett Favre twice and had begun to escape Favre's enormous shadow.

were still learning exactly how to play without Finley and Grant, two of their most vital weapons. In addition, the injuries kept piling up. Outside linebacker Brad Jones injured his shoulder and went on injured reserve after the Minnesota game. Brady Poppinga, Jones' backup, also suffered a knee injury against Miami and went on I.R.

But the Packers were learning to overcome such adversity and finding a way to win in the process. The victory over Minnesota gave the Packers an enormous shot of confidence and a real belief that they could turn around a season that hadn't always gone as hoped. Green Bay played with a poise and coolness the following week and upset the New York Jets, 9–0.

The Jets had entered the game a six-point favorite, but Green Bay forced three turnovers and blanked Rex Ryan's bombastic bunch. New York, widely considered the AFC's top team, had been humbled on their home field, and the Packers were once again riding high. "We love to be underdogs," Packers safety Nick Collins said. "Everybody thinks the Jets are the team to win the Super Bowl. We wanted to come in here and match their

Rodgers and the Green Bay offense struggled against the Jets in New York, but the defense was stellar in recording a 9–0 shutout.

intensity and show them that we can play with anybody."

Green Bay was just getting started. One week later, with a national television audience watching, the Packers played one of their finest games in McCarthy's five-year tenure. Green Bay dominated in every facet and routed Dallas, 45–7, on Sunday Night Football.

"[The Packers] whipped us about every way you could whip somebody," said Cowboys coach Wade Phillips, who was fired the following day. "They're a good football team playing at home, and they played well, and we didn't play well at all. That's the way the game went."

Green Bay's offense finally hit its stride, as well. The Packers rolled up 415 yards of total offense, their second-highest total of the season. Green Bay had a season-high 26 first downs and converted a season-best 66.7 percent of its third downs (10-of-15).

Rodgers threw for 289 yards and three touchdowns, completed 79.4 percent of his passes and had a 131.5 passer rating, the third-highest total of his career. Wideout James Jones set career highs in catches (eight) and yards (123). And the

Rodgers' arms and legs were too much for the Cowboys on November 7, 2010. The Packers' 45–7 rout cost Dallas coach Wade Phillips his job the next day.

AP Images

Packers ran for 138 yards, their second-highest total of the year.

"I think we had a good plan," said Rodgers, who had his highest passer rating of the season. "We just got into a flow early. I think I haven't played this kind of game really this season yet. I'm playing the way I feel like I'm capable of playing. It was nice to play better. It was obviously a combination of a number of things, but Mike [McCarthy] called some very high-percentage plays early in the game for me, and I feel like I really got into a rhythm early."

Green Bay was heading to its bye week with a 6–3 record and a three-game winning streak. The first stretch of the season was far more challenging than anyone would have imagined, but somehow, Rodgers and the Packers had survived. "It gives us momentum going into the bye week," Woodson said of the dominating win. "We have some time off, which slows us down a little bit, but hopefully we come back in a couple weeks ready to go, and have that same intensity."

They did. In its first game after the bye week, Green Bay went to Minnesota to face a Vikings team on the brink of collapse. By the time things had ended, Minnesota had undoubtedly crumpled. Rodgers was virtually flawless, throwing for 301 yards and four touchdowns, including three to Jennings. Favre had another rough day, and the Packers routed their border-state rivals, 31–3. "This has got me at a loss for words," Favre said afterward. "Disappointing would be an understatement."

One day later, Vikings owner Zigi Wilf fired head coach Brad Childress. It marked the second time in as many games that the Packers' rout of an opponent led to the dismissal of their head coach. "We've got a foot on the gas, hands on the wheel, and we're looking straight ahead," McCarthy said. Twelve months earlier, the Packers couldn't solve Favre and the Vikings. Now, in less than a month, Green Bay had vanquished them both twice.

The Packers were suddenly the hottest team in the NFC, thanks to a four-game winning streak in which their average margin of victory was 19.8 points. Green Bay (7–3) was tied for first place in the NFC North and on its way to Atlanta (8–2) for a shot at first place in the conference. "We're a good football team; we always knew we were a good football

Aaron Rodgers scrambles away from Atlanta's John Abraham during a Week 12 showdown. The Falcons rallied late, though, to post a 20–17 win.

team," McCarthy said. "We'll crank it up and get ready for Atlanta."

The Packers' trip to the Georgia Dome didn't go as hoped. Atlanta's Matt Bryant kicked a 47-yard field goal with just nine seconds left, and the Falcons prevailed, 20–17. The loss was a major blow to the Packers' hopes of having homefield advantage throughout the post-season. "It's discouraging not to win a game we should have won," Rodgers said.

Rodgers did all he could. Green Bay's running game was in hibernation again, so McCarthy put the offense in his quarterback's hands. Rodgers threw for 344 yards and led the Packers on a memorable 90-yard, game-tying drive in the final minute. On fourth-and-goal from the Atlanta 10, Rodgers fired a dart to Jordy Nelson that tied the game, 17–17.

"You go down and score a touchdown, and you're thinking overtime," said Rodgers, who also had a critical fumble at the goal line in the second quarter. "Tying the game was pretty special." But after a 40-yard kick return by Atlanta's Eric Weems and a face-mask penalty on Green Bay's Matt Wilhelm, the Falcons needed to go just 20 yards for the winning kick.

Atlanta was now 9–2 and in control of the NFC race. The Packers had dropped to 7–4 and had fallen behind Chicago in the NFC North. "I have no plans of going to Lambeau Field in January," Falcons wideout Roddy White said. "I plan on staying right here and sleeping in my own bed in the playoffs." White would eventually get his wish. The Packers, meanwhile, again had work to do.

It started with an impressive 34–16 dismantling of San Francisco. The 49ers had passed on Rodgers at the top of the 2005 draft, and there was nothing he enjoyed better than making them pay. Rodgers did exactly that on this day, throwing three TD passes—including two to Greg Jennings—and for 298 total yards. Interestingly, the 49ers were still searching for a suitable quarterback. Alex Smith, the player San Francisco selected instead of Rodgers at No. 1, had fizzled. And the 49ers were now using journeyman Troy Smith.

"I think every player, particularly quarterbacks, the path that you're put on has a lot to do with your success," McCarthy said when talking of Rodgers and Smith. "There's a lot of factors that go into developing a quarterback. Obviously they both had unique ability to even be considered to be part of the conversation of being the No. 1 pick in the National Football League."

This was the latest example, though, of how the 49ers would have given anything to have that pick back. Rodgers threw TD passes of 57 yards and 1 yard to Jennings. Driver also caught a 61-yard TD that will forever be part of the Packers' 2010 highlight reel.

On Green Bay's opening drive of the second half and the Packers facing a second-and-16 at their own 39, Driver lined up in the right slot. He found a hole in San Francisco's zone and hauled in a strike from Rodgers at the 49ers' 38. Driver spun away from safety Reggie Smith at the 30, then ducked under a tackle attempt by safety Dashon Goldson at the 22. Cornerback Nate Clements had an angle on Driver, but Driver simply shoved him out of the way at the 10.

Three 49ers finally corralled Driver at the 4, but he dragged them into the right corner of the end zone for an improbable 61-yard TD and a 21–13 Green Bay lead. "Donald made one of the most amazing catches and runs I've ever seen," Rodgers said. "We nicknamed him 'The Kickstand.'

That's been his nickname around here since I've been here. When he was at about the 20, I was thinking, 'Go down, go down, don't get drilled,' and then when he broke another tackle I was hoping he'd get it in the end zone."

The game also marked the debut of rookie running back James Starks, who spent the first 12 weeks of the year either inactive or on the physically-unable-to-perform list. But Starks proved worth the wait, rushing for 73 yards on 18 carries in his season debut. "I was just keeping my eyes open," Starks said. "Whatever was asked of me, I was ready for it. I prepared well in practice and was just ready for the opportunity."

With a quarter of the regular season remaining, the Packers also appeared ready to make their move. Instead, all of their best-laid plans were swept away the following week after a shocking 7–3 loss in Detroit. Rodgers was knocked out of the game in the second quarter with his second concussion of the year. Green Bay's offense had been brutal with Rodgers and also struggled with backup Matt Flynn.

And when Lions third-string quarterback Drew Stanton threw a fourth-quarter

TD to tight end Will Heller, Detroit snapped a 19-game losing streak to their NFC North foes. "I can't really measure the level of a concussion at this point," McCarthy said afterward in regard to Rodgers. "He'll go through the normal protocol this week. I was just told that his head is clear, and he has a headache."

Green Bay's season was undeniably at a crossroads. The Packers had now lost two of three and were on the outside looking in at the playoff race. Rodgers would miss Green Bay's next game in New England. And the Packers' final three opponents were a combined 29–10 (.744), giving the Packers the toughest remaining schedule in football.

The first team on that murderer's row was mighty New England, winners of five straight and boasting an NFL-best 11–2 record. Although Green Bay entered the game a 14-point underdog, McCarthy wasn't treating this as a David vs. Goliath affair. "We're nobody's underdog," McCarthy boldly proclaimed. "We have all the confidence in our abilities. We've had challenges throughout the season. We've stepped up to those challenges, and we feel the same way going into this game."

One will never know if that was false bravado or not. New England's last three wins had been by an average of 30.7 points. But the Packers certainly didn't play like anybody's underdog. Backup quarterback Matt Flynn played extremely well subbing for Rodgers and threw three TD passes. Flynn also drove the Packers to the Patriots' 15-yard line in the closing seconds, but he was sacked on the final play of the game.

Despite the defeat, the Packers left Foxboro that night fully believing in themselves once again. If they could go blow-for-blow with arguably football's best team—and do it without Rodgers—they could play with anybody, right? "I think that was a huge point in our season for our confidence," Driver said. "We didn't win the game. But after that game, we knew we could play with anybody again."

On that same Sunday, the Packers caught an enormous break when Philadelphia's DeSean Jackson returned a punt 65 yards on the final play of the game to lift the Eagles past the New York Giants, 38–31. The Eagles (10–4) were likely headed to the playoffs regardless of that outcome. But with the Giants (9–5)

Rodgers was aided by a rejuvenated running attack in leading Green Bay to a 34–16 trouncing of the 49ers in Week 13.

losing and coming to Lambeau Field the following week, the Packers once again controlled their own postseason fate.

"Our playoffs started when we got on the plane to come home," McCarthy said. "That's the way we're approaching our preparation, that's the way we're approaching this game. It's going to be a playoff-type atmosphere here at home." The key to everything, of course, was Rodgers. By Tuesday, Rodgers was cleared to play. He then proceeded to have one of the best games of his young life.

Rodgers threw for a career-high 404 yards, tied a personal best with four touchdown passes, and posted the third-highest passer rating of his career (139.9). The result was a stunning 45–17 rout of the New York Giants that put the Packers back in control of their playoff destiny.

"It was fun," Rodgers said. "I had a good week of preparation this week. I think that's kind of where it started. I felt good throwing the ball all week, liked the game plan, liked the things we were trying to do, and once we were into the game, I liked the rhythm that Mike [McCarthy] had our offense in."

Rodgers switched to a new helmet that had additional padding. The goal was to lower the risk of another concussion, but because Rodgers' face was jammed into the helmet, he took a lot of grief from teammates. While Rodgers' face may have looked funny, there was nothing comical about his arm.

"I felt all week a lot of energy," Rodgers said. "My arm felt like it was live. I threw the ball really good in practice, so I had a lot of confidence going into the game that I was going to perform this way—obviously, not maybe as well as it went—but I think you can contribute that to some really good play calls at certain times and some big plays by some guys."

One of the few tense moments came late in the first quarter, when Rodgers took off running. As the Lambeau Field faithful held their collective breath, Rodgers picked up 15 yards and then slid before getting walloped. Rodgers proceeded to jump up and signal "safe." At that moment, the sellout crowd went berserk. It was only the start, as Rodgers shredded the Giants' secondary and put the Packers back on track for a playoff berth.

"We were ready to play," Jennings said. "We prepared all week with the focus

After missing a game and a half because of a concussion, Rodgers returned to form in spectacular fashion against the Giants. He passed for a career-high 404 yards in leading the Packers to a 45–17 victory.

and mind-set of this is it—this is our season. In front of this crowd and in our own backyard, we can't go down like that. We came out here and gave it our best shot, and it was a great shot today."

Only one test remained: the archrival Chicago Bears. While the Bears had already clinched the NFC North title and a first-round bye, they wanted nothing more than to knock their oldest rival out of the postseason. That's why Chicago coach Lovie Smith played his starters the entire way, even though theoretically, the Bears had nothing to gain with a win. "We're playing to win the game," Smith insisted.

And Chicago did throughout the memorable 181st tussle between these teams. But Rodgers hit tight end Donald Lee with a 1-yard TD pass early in the fourth quarter to give the Packers a thrilling 10–3 win. "It feels incredible," said Packers outside linebacker Erik Walden, who had a career day with 2.5 sacks and 16 tackles. "It didn't always look great for us, but we got it done."

The Packers got it done thanks to a terrific defensive effort that limited the Bears to 227 total yards and just 97 after halftime.

Green Bay sacked Bears quarterback Jay Cutler six times, had two interceptions, and limited Cutler to a 43.5 passer rating—less than half his season average. "I don't know if it was our best [defensive] game this year or not," Packers nose tackle B.J. Raji said. "But if it wasn't, it was close."

Green Bay's win gave it the sixth and final NFC playoff berth and knocked the New York Giants out of the postseason. The Packers, Giants, and Tampa Bay all finished with 10–6 records, but Green Bay won the tiebreaker based on strength of victory.

Afterward, the Packers were elated to have overcome an inordinate number of injuries to reach the postseason. As Chicago's bus rolled out of Lambeau Field that frigid night, many Bears had a different thought. "I kept thinking we're going to see them again," Bears cornerback Tim Jennings said of the Packers. "I was thinking, 'Man, we should have knocked them out.'"

Jennings didn't know how right he was. ■

After yet another must-win victory—this one 10–3 over the Bears—a relieved Aaron Rodgers trots off Lambeau Field en route to his second foray into the playoffs.

CHAPTER 9

RETURN TO THE PLAYOFFS

Green Bay's postseason almost ended as quickly as it began. Thanks to Tramon Williams, the Packers' run to greatness was only getting started. The Packers had controlled play throughout much of their Wild Card game in Philadelphia. They had been sharp on offense early, stout on defense throughout, and led the entire way. But late in the contest, the Eagles closed to within 21–16 and had driven to Green Bay's 27-yard line.

On first-and-10, Eagles quarterback Michael Vick faked a throw down the middle and then threw for rookie Riley Cooper in the left corner of the end zone. Williams never bit on the ball fake, though, and had perfect position to intercept Vick's pass with 33 seconds left and send the Packers to the NFC Divisional Game. "I feel like I got greedy and took a shot at the end zone,"

Vick said. "I didn't throw the ball I wanted and got picked. It's not the way I wanted to go out, but I went down swinging."

Aaron Rodgers was swinging throughout, as well, and became the first Packers quarterback other than Brett Favre to win a postseason game since Lynn Dickey on January 8, 1983. Rodgers threw three touchdowns, completed 66.7 percent of his 27 passes, and had a lights-out passer rating of 122.5.

Rodgers had been criticized in some circles throughout 2010 for never winning a playoff game. Of course, he'd only had one opportunity and helped the 2009 Packers score 45 points at Arizona. "Well, in all my time being a football fan I have never seen one player win a game all by himself," Rodgers said. "It is a good team win for us, and I will let you guys

Aaron Rodgers had three touchdown passes and a 122.5 passer rating as the Packers defeated Philadelphia 21–16 in their NFC Wild Card game.

"I'M PROBABLY BIASED, BUT I THINK AARON RODGERS IS PROBABLY AS GOOD AN IN-AND-OUT-OF-THE-POCKET QUARTERBACK AS THERE IS IN FOOTBALL TODAY. —Mike McCarthy

write what you want on that."

Rodgers was huge as the Packers jumped on the Eagles early. He threw a seven-yard TD pass to tight end Tom Crabtree—the first of Crabtree's career—and a nine-yard score to James Jones as Green Bay jumped out to a 14–0 lead. After the Eagles closed to within 14–10 early in the third quarter, Rodgers threw a screen pass to running back Brandon Jackson that he took 16 yards for a TD.

"I'm probably biased, but I think Aaron Rodgers is probably as good an in-and-out-of-the-pocket quarterback as there is in football today," Packers coach Mike McCarthy said. "His ability to play in the pocket, trusting his footwork, the time clock, the ability to come out of the pocket to buy time, that's Aaron's strength.

"And on top of that ... he has the arm strength to make all of the throws. It gives you a lot of versatility as a play-caller and as an offensive schemer when you have a quarterback right now with his experience, playing as well as he is. He's a special player."

To the surprise of the football world, Packers rookie running back James Starks was extremely special on this afternoon, as well. Starks, who had just 101 rushing yards during the regular season, erupted for 123 yards on 23 carries. Starks' total established a Packers rookie postseason record, breaking the old mark of 88 yards held by Travis "The Roadrunner" Williams set in 1967. Starks' output was also the highest by a Green Bay running back in 2010, topping Brandon Jackson's 115-yard effort against Washington in Week 5.

"The way that James Starks was

Green Bay had never won a playoff game in Philadelphia until Rodgers & Co. did so in the 2010 postseason.

running the ball tonight was maybe one of the most important factors in this win," Rodgers said. "He ran great, and I am so happy for him. He is a great kid, and he has really grown a lot in the past couple weeks. He was big tonight."

In the end, though, it came down to Green Bay's defense. And thanks to Williams, the Packers were moving on. "Tramon Williams has clearly played at a Pro Bowl level, there's no question about it," McCarthy said. "Tramon Williams, he has done it all year; he has been playing at this level all year." Williams was just getting started. So was Rodgers.

Atlanta, the NFC's No. 1 seed that had gone 13–3 during the regular season, was about to pay the price. The Falcons entered their NFC Divisional Playoff game against Green Bay with two full weeks of rest. The Falcons were extremely confident after defeating the Packers in their own building just two months earlier.

But on a memorable Saturday night for Packer Nation, the Rodgers-Williams duo was beyond dynamic and led Green Bay to a 48–21 destruction of the Falcons. Rodgers, making just his third postseason start, had a game for the ages in the Georgia Dome. He completed 31 of 36 passes for

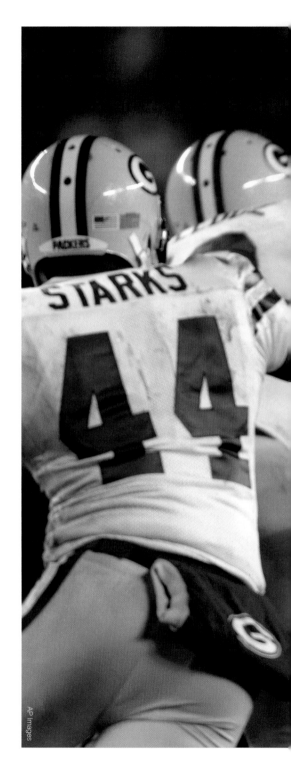

James Starks (44) set a Packers' rookie postseason rushing record with 123 yards against the Eagles.

366 yards, three touchdowns, no interceptions, and posted a passer rating of 136.8.

Williams had two interceptions in a two-and-a-half-minute window late in the first half. The first stopped a potential Falcons touchdown, while Williams went 70 yards with the second interception for a game-changing touchdown. "To see your big-time players step up in the prime-time games, that's what it's all about," Packers coach Mike McCarthy said.

The Packers were dominant on both sides of the ball throughout. But no one stepped up more than Rodgers or Williams. Rodgers' performance against Atlanta was arguably the greatest postseason game ever by a Packers quarterback and one of the finest in NFL history.

Rodgers set Packers playoff records for completions (31) and completion percentage (86.1 percent) and had the second-most passing yardage in team history (366). In 10 possessions, Rodgers led Green Bay to five touchdowns, two field goals, and the Packers never punted. "This probably was my best performance—the stage we were on, the importance of this game," Rodgers

said afterward. "It was a good night."

Rodgers threw touchdown passes to Jordy Nelson (6 yards), James Jones (20), and John Kuhn (7). Rodgers was razor sharp, shredded what had been a respectable defense, and got plenty of help from his gifted wideouts. The most impressive part of Rodgers' night, though, might have been his feet. On several plays, Atlanta standout defensive end John Abraham seemed ready to dump Rodgers. But the nifty quarterback escaped and even had a seven-yard TD run.

Williams, on the other hand, just doesn't make bad plays. Instead, he makes game-changing ones, and thanks to his memorable playoff performances, he was becoming a household name. One week after notching the game-saving interception in Philadelphia, Williams was even better against the Falcons.

With the game tied at 14 late in the second quarter, Falcons quarterback Matt Ryan took a shot to the end zone for 6-foot-4 wideout Michael Jenkins. But the 5-foot-11 Williams played the ball better, and when Jenkins lost his footing,

Aaron Rodgers had a game for the ages (31-of-36, 366 yards, three TDs) as the Packers hammered No. 1 seed Atlanta 48–21 in the NFC Divisional playoffs.

Rodgers scrambles around Falcons linebacker Curtis Lofton for a seven-yard touchdown run during the second half of the Packers' playoff rout of Atlanta.

Williams went up and picked Ryan off with 2:20 left in the first half.

"I think we have lots of guys on the defense that can make those plays," Williams said. "I think I've just been put in that position the last couple of weeks and made those plays for my teammates. I don't see it as a big deal." Oh, it was a big deal. And right before the half, Williams made a play that was an even bigger deal.

Green Bay had taken a 21–14 lead, but Atlanta was driving into field-goal range and had reached the Packers' 35. With just 10 seconds left in the half, Ryan rolled left and threw back across his body for Roddy White. Williams jumped the route, though, made a nifty cut past Ryan at midfield, and then sailed to the end zone to make it 28–14.

When the Packers scored on their first drive of the third quarter to make it 35–14, this one was essentially over. "I think everything he's done, every good thing that's happened to Tramon on the field, all the plays he's making he deserves," Packers linebacker A.J. Hawk said of Williams. "I've never been around

probably a better teammate than a guy like Tramon. He's awesome. I love how he prepares. He does everything right."

Against the Falcons, both Rodgers and Williams did virtually everything right. Now, it was on to Chicago with a Super Bowl berth at stake. Just three weeks earlier, the Bears had a chance to end Green Bay's season. Now, Chicago was wishing it had done exactly that.

Although the Bears had homefield, Green Bay was coming to Soldier Field as arguably football's hottest team. And even though the Packers finished second to Chicago in the NFC North and were going on the road, Green Bay was installed as a three-point favorite.

"It's going to be backyard football," said Bears defensive end Israel Idonije. "Man on man. They throw a punch, we throw a punch. We're going to slug back and forth, and the first one to flinch or drop is going to lose the game."

This would be the 182nd meeting in this storied rivalry. Amazingly, though, these bitter adversaries had played just once in the postseason. That came in 1941,

Aaron Rodgers and Bears middle linebacker Brian Urlacher (54) both had their moments during the NFC Championship Game.

when George Halas' Bears defeated Curly Lambeau's Packers, 33–14, in a Western Division playoff game played at Wrigley Field in Chicago.

The two fan bases were in a frenzy beforehand. So were the teams. "I think it takes the rivalry to the next level," Rodgers said. "It's great that there's so much history, the longest-running rivalry in the National Football League. To have one of us, the winner of this game, go to the Super Bowl is pretty special."

It was even more special a few days later when Rodgers and his teammates were presented the Halas Trophy after their 21–14 win over Chicago in the NFC Championship Game. Green Bay was far from perfect, failing to score an offensive point after taking a 14–0 lead early in the second quarter. But the Packers got a big day from their defense and notched the franchise's biggest win in 13 years.

"We would have liked to put more than 14 points on the board, obviously, but we're going to the Super Bowl," Rodgers said. "We've got a week to relax and get our bodies back and go enjoy Dallas and hopefully get a win down there." The way the Packers started against the Bears, it looked like they'd breeze to Dallas.

Aaron Rodgers led the Packers on a seven-play, 84-yard touchdown march on their first possession of the NFC Championship Game. The Packers would never trail.

On Green Bay's first drive, Rodgers led a seven-play, 84-yard march that he capped with a one-yard TD run. Rodgers was 4-for-4 on the drive for 76 yards and hit Greg Jennings twice for 48 yards. "Frankly, the first drive was the way we anticipated coming into this game," McCarthy said. "I thought we were able to get into a tremendous rhythm."

Green Bay stayed in rhythm and went ahead, 14–0, just four minutes into the second quarter. The Packers needed only five plays to cover 44 yards on that drive. Running back Brandon Jackson (16 yards) and wideout Jordy Nelson (15) both had big catches on the march, and running back James Starks finished the deal with a four-yard TD run.

"The way we started out, I thought we were going to put up 40 points on [Chicago]," Packers right guard Josh Sitton said. "We came out and were running good, throwing good, just rolling like Atlanta." Yes, for a little more than a quarter, this felt exactly like the NFC Divisional Playoffs, when the Packers drilled the Falcons, 48–21. From that point forward,

though, everything changed.

In Green Bay's first four possessions, it rolled up 181 total yards, had 12 first downs, and averaged 7.9 yards per play. In the Packers' final 10 possessions, they had 175 total yards, 11 first downs, and averaged just 3.9 yards per play. "It was weird, man," Packers wideout James Jones said. "We don't feel like there's anybody out there that can stop us except us. And the rest of the game, I'd just say we stopped ourselves."

Fortunately for Green Bay, though, its defense stole the show. The Packers forced three turnovers, held Chicago's three quarterbacks to a combined passer rating of 45.2, and allowed just 132 total yards through three quarters. "It seems the defense has put these last three games away," linebacker Clay Matthews said. "We had our backs against the wall a little bit, but we made the play to win the game."

Leading the charge were undrafted rookie cornerback Sam Shields and second-year nose tackle B.J. Raji. Shields had a pair of interceptions, including one with 37 seconds left and Chicago driving for the

Chicago linebacker Brian Urlacher had a huge second-half interception against Aaron Rodgers. But Rodgers made an even bigger play by tackling Urlacher and saving a touchdown.

potential game-tying score. Raji bailed out Green Bay's struggling offense with an 18-yard interception return for a touchdown midway through the fourth quarter.

"It's an unbelievable feeling," said Shields, who entered the game with two interceptions all year. "There's a lot of guys that wait a long, long time for this. Now, we're going to the Super Bowl." Shields was a major reason why. Late in the first half the Bears trailed, 14–0, but had seized momentum after Lance Briggs intercepted Rodgers. Two plays later, Chicago quarterback Jay Cutler took a shot down the left sideline for wideout Johnny Knox.

Shields, who played wideout for three years at the University of Miami, ran stride for stride with Knox, then turned and almost became the receiver. Shields had inside leverage, got to the ball before Knox, and made a gorgeous pick. "I just got my head around and went to the highest point," said Shields, who also had a sack. Shields' second interception was the biggest play he's made as a Packer.

Chicago third-string quarterback Caleb Hanie had rallied the Bears to within 21–14 late in the fourth quarter. Chicago had driven to Green Bay's 29-yard line, had a fourth-and-5, and still had 47 seconds to notch the equalizer. Hanie

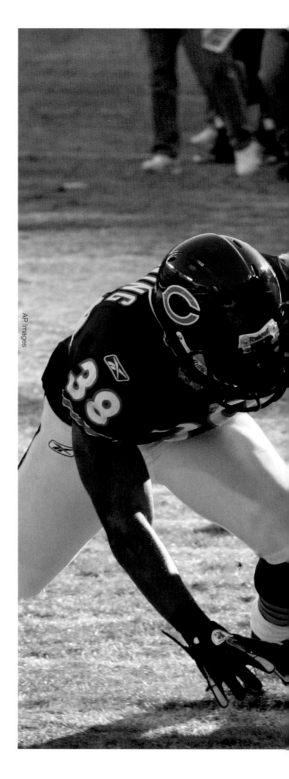

Aaron Rodgers didn't have any touchdown passes in the NFC Championship Game, but he did run for one score.

worked out of the shotgun, the Bears sent out four receivers, and the Packers rushed five. Hanie took a shot down the middle for Knox, but Shields jumped the route knowing safety Nick Collins was providing help from behind.

With his coaches screaming, 'Get down,' Shields returned the interception 32 yards. When Shields rose up, he was mobbed by teammates that knew their next stop was the Super Bowl. "We need to work on that last play, getting on the ground a little sooner," Packers coach Mike McCarthy joked. "Sam, for a rookie—and I told a couple other rookies this—you have no idea what you've accomplished here in your first year in the league. He is going to be a great player for the Green Bay Packers for a long time."

Raji certainly fit that bill, as well. With the Packers clinging to a 14–7 lead midway through the fourth quarter, Raji made a play that McCarthy called a "game-winner." The Bears had a third-and-5 from their own 15. Raji lined up over center Olin Kreutz, showed blitz, and then dropped into the middle of the field where Hanie was trying to get the ball to running back Matt Forte.

Hanie never saw Raji and threw the ball right into his enormous mitts. Raji caught the ball naturally and then waltzed to the right corner of the end zone to make it 21–7. Raji didn't have an interception in the NFL or college, so his timing was ideal for Packer Nation. "It's just a great feeling," Raji said. "It was a great call. I was behind the back, and obviously he wasn't expecting that. I just caught it and ran it back."

The play was one of the most memorable in Packers playoff history. And now, Green Bay was headed back to the Super Bowl for the first time since 1997, where it would face AFC giant Pittsburgh.

"I'm numb," said McCarthy, who grew up in Pittsburgh and was an assistant coach at the University of Pittsburgh from 1989 to 1992. "It's a great feeling. I'm just so proud of our football team. As I said, we have a goal of playing 16 quarters, and we've completed 12. We're fired up and getting ready to go to Dallas, Texas."

Getting ready for the time of their lives. ■

A tired Aaron Rodgers was all smiles after leading the Green Bay Packers past Chicago, 21–14, in the NFC Championship Game.

CHAPTER 10

CHAMPIONS OF THE FOOTBALL WORLD

Experience. As Super Bowl XLV approached, experience was the buzzword. The Pittsburgh Steelers had tons of it. The Green Bay Packers had very little. Would it make a difference? "When we get into the game, then it's just the Super Bowl," Packers fullback John Kuhn insisted. "It's the Super Bowl and the event that nobody has really experienced. The game is still the game."

The Packers were hoping that was true, because the Steelers' roster was dotted with past Super Bowl standouts. From Ben Roethlisberger to James Harrison to Hines Ward, Pittsburgh entered the world's biggest sporting event with a "been there, done that" attitude. In all, Pittsburgh had 14 starters that won a Super Bowl championship. The Steelers also had 10 players with two rings and a

total of 25 players that had competed in a Super Bowl.

The Packers had not been to a Super Bowl since 1997. And the only Packers to ever play in a Super Bowl were cornerback Charles Woodson and defensive end Ryan Pickett, and both played on losing teams. Green Bay insisted, though, that once the ball was kicked, none of that would matter.

"I look at it like the hungry dog hunts harder than the fat dog," said Packers tight end Donald Lee. "And we have a lot of hungry dogs in this locker room that are willing to do whatever it takes to win that game. I'm sure they're willing to do what it takes, too, but if I was a betting man, I'd bet my money on the hungry dog."

This was Pittsburgh's third Super Bowl appearance in six years. The Steelers defeated Seattle and Arizona in the

Aaron Rodgers and the Green Bay Packers couldn't match the championship-game experience of Pittsburgh entering Super Bowl XLV, but in the end, it didn't seem to matter.

"WE'RE GOING TO HANDLE OUR BUSINESS, STAY CALM AND COOL, AND EVERYTHING WILL WORK OUT. —Brandon Jackson

40th and 43rd Super Bowls, respectively, and many of the key cogs from those teams still remained. Ward was the MVP of Super Bowl XL after catching five passes for 123 yards and a touchdown. Harrison had a 100-yard interception return for a touchdown in Super Bowl XLIII. And Roethlisberger was the winning quarterback in each of those games.

Others, like Pro Bowl safety Troy Polamalu, mammoth nose tackle Casey Hampton, steady tight end Heath Miller, and splendid linebackers LaMarr Woodley, James Farrior, and Larry Foote, all played a role in Pittsburgh's recent success. Even 38-year-old head coach Mike Tomlin, in his fourth year, had a Super Bowl win on his résumé. "It's meaningful," Packers head coach Mike McCarthy admitted. "But we're aware of it and understand that we haven't been there before, and that's something we'll talk about and make sure expectations and responsibilities [are] clear for everybody."

Green Bay's Super Bowl experience was less impressive. Kuhn was on the Steelers' practice squad in 2005 and got a ring after Pittsburgh beat Seattle in Super Bowl XL Kuhn never played in that game, though. Pickett was a rookie with St. Louis in 2001 when the Rams lost to New England in Super Bowl XXXVI. And Woodson was part of Oakland's 2002 team that was routed by Tampa Bay in Super Bowl XXXVII.

"I believe if we stay calm and stay cool and understand what's going on, everything will work out," Packers running back Brandon Jackson said. "We've been on the big stage before, not as big as this, but as far as playoffs and everything like that, we've been on that type of stage. We're going to handle our business, stay calm and cool, and everything will work out."

The Packers agreed that Pittsburgh's

During Super Bowl week, Aaron Rodgers answered a wide array of questions and just tried to avoid giving the Steelers any bulletin-board material.

experience could be an advantage in the days leading up to the game. Super Bowl week is packed with potential distractions, and that experience was going to be new to most of Green Bay's players. But the Packers also believed that once kickoff arrived, it was just back to football.

"The biggest thing is ... trying to manage your schedule and keep it as similar as you can to what it would be like in a normal week," quarterback Aaron Rodgers said. "There's going to be a bunch of different things pulling at you ... There's going to be a lot of different things that could disrupt your week if you let them."

Green Bay's week was fantastically quiet, though, which is just what head coach Mike McCarthy and his staff hoped for. The Packers had a mini-controversy shortly before Super Bowl week on whether or not the 15 players on injured reserve would be included in the team picture. Eventually they were, and that issue was settled before Green Bay got to Dallas.

Roethlisberger actually made the most noise in the days leading up to the game. The Steelers' quarterback was seen at a karaoke bar in Fort Worth, Texas, belting out Billy Joel's "Piano Man" and several other songs on the Tuesday of Super Bowl week. "Tuesday night I take

Rodgers and his Packers teammates were relaxed and confident as they waited in the tunnel at Cowboys Stadium prior to the kickoff of Super Bowl XLV.

Jim Biever

my linemen out to dinner, and we went to a great barbeque spot," Roethlisberger said. "We went there and wanted to listen to some live music, so we went to a piano bar. We just had an enjoyable night."

Rodgers, on the other hand, did the exact opposite. "I haven't been out carousing," he said. "I am a homebody so I've been spending a lot of time in my hotel room watching film. I think it is important at the same time that you are sticking with your normal routine. I like to go out to dinner when I'm back home in Green Bay so I've gone out to dinner, to a couple of really nice spots, and then come home, relax, and watch film."

In general, though, the week was largely anticlimactic. The Steelers changed hotels on Saturday to avoid distractions. The Packers stayed put. Green Bay held a chapel session Saturday at 8:30 PM and had a 9:00 PM team meeting. But when all of the speeches and pep talks had ended, McCarthy made perhaps his boldest decision of the 2010 season.

He told his team to go and get fitted for Super Bowl rings. Amazingly, McCarthy had that on the team's itinerary for Saturday night. "I talked to our football team a lot about having real confidence, and those are just examples and opportunities to express that," said McCarthy, who was born and raised in Pittsburgh. "I felt that the measurement of the rings, the timing of it would be special, it would have a significant effect on our players doing it the night before the game.

"Scheduling is so important during the course of the week, and you want to do certain things at certain times, and I felt that was the appropriate time. I thought it would be special. I thought it would give us a boost of confidence to do it the night before the game."

When game day arrived, Green Bay's collective confidence couldn't have been higher. McCarthy built his offensive game plan around Rodgers, who had shredded these same Steelers just 14 months earlier. McCarthy loved the matchups of his receivers against Pittsburgh's secondary, and now it was up to Green Bay's line to protect and for Rodgers to deliver. "A huge part of our game plan was really putting the ball in Aaron Rodgers' hands," McCarthy said.

Defensively, the emergence of Packers cornerbacks Tramon Williams and Sam Shields had Green Bay's secondary in far better shape than 2009. The Steelers had also dealt standout receiver Santonio Holmes away the previous offseason and were thin behind starters Mike Wallace and Hines Ward.

Steelers running back Rashard Mendenhall had emerged as a force in his third season and would be a huge challenge for Green Bay's mediocre run defense. In the end, though, the Packers fully believed the game would be decided by one category. "We have to not turn the ball over," Rodgers said. "This team thrives on forcing turnovers, and if we can hang on to the football and not turn it over we are going to have a good chance to win."

Less than 12 minutes into the game, the Packers' chances of victory had increased exponentially. On Green Bay's second possession of a scoreless game, Rodgers went to work on the Steelers secondary. Sharp, accurate, rhythmic, Rodgers hooked up twice with wideout Jordy Nelson for 18 total yards and brilliantly avoided pressure to find Brandon Jackson for 14 yards.

The Packers had driven to the Steelers' 29-yard line, when on third-and-1, they lined up with two tight ends and Nelson the lone receiver split far right. Pittsburgh anticipated a run, and that left

Nelson one-on-one with mediocre cornerback William Gay.

Gay came to the line to play press coverage, but Nelson beat him by faking inside and then releasing down the right sideline. The Packers' offensive line did their jobs, and then Rodgers lofted a perfect fade to the right corner of the end zone. Nelson had a step on Gay and won a hand-fighting battle between the two. Nelson then hauled in Rodgers' gorgeous toss to give the Packers a 7–0 lead with 3:44 left in the first quarter.

"It was just press (coverage)," Nelson said. "Aaron gave me a little signal if it was press to go deep. It was actually a screen play, but he checked to a go route. That's what we hit." Green Bay's hitting had only begun.

Pittsburgh began its next drive on its own 7-yard line after an illegal block penalty. And on the first play, Roethlisberger made perhaps the game's biggest blunder. Green Bay rushed just four, but Roethlisberger was trying to hit a home run to Wallace so he needed substantial time for the play to develop. That allowed beefy defensive end Howard Green, who was signed off the street in October when the Packers were ravaged by injury, to get home.

Green whipped left guard Chris Kemoeatu and then drilled Roethlisberger as he let loose a bomb for Wallace. Green's pressure caused Roethlisberger's pass to be severely underthrown, and Packers safety Nick Collins intercepted. Collins, who has been named to three straight Pro Bowls, took off down the right sideline and made a nifty cut back inside. When Collins reached the 3-yard line, he jumped and reached the end zone.

In a matter of 24 seconds, Green Bay had surged to a 14–0 lead. "Oh man, that was the highlight of my day right there," Collins said. "I was able to read Big Ben [Roethlisberger] and got a nice jump on the ball. I made a couple cuts to get into the end zone." Rodgers had stressed all week that turnovers would determine a winner. And late in the first half, he was beginning to look prophetic.

With the Packers leading, 14–3, Pittsburgh was on the move. Operating out of the shotgun, Roethlisberger threw a short pass over the middle for Wallace, but cornerback Jarrett Bush read the crossing route, drove on the ball, and picked it off. Bush, one of the more maligned players in recent Packers history, developed into a special teams stalwart in 2010. But this was undoubtedly the biggest play he made

Aaron Rodgers and the Packers were brimming with confidence throughout Super Bowl week.

170

from scrimmage during his five years in Green Bay.

"You know what, you've got to give them a lot of credit," Roethlisberger said. "They're a great defense; they got after us, and I turned the ball over, and you can't do that." Especially with a quarterback like Rodgers on the other side.

Green Bay started on its own 47, and on its second play, Rodgers hit Nelson for 16 yards against nickel corner Bryant McFadden. Two plays later, Rodgers made one of his finest throws as a Packer. On a first-and-10 from Pittsburgh's 21, the Packers lined up four wide receivers; the Steelers rushed four and dropped seven. Greg Jennings lined up in the left slot and ran a deep seam route.

Jennings had gotten behind linebacker James Farrior and in front of safety Ryan Clark, but Rodgers' window was small, and his pass had to be perfect. It was. Rodgers delivered a dart that Clark missed by inches. Jennings took a wicked shot from safety Troy Polamalu, but he was already in the end zone.

The Packers led, 21–3, with just more than two minutes remaining in the first half. Things couldn't be going any better.

"It was like they were a hair faster than we were all night," Clark said. Shortly before halftime, though, the Steelers were given new life.

At the two-minute mark, Shields left with a shoulder injury. Shields would return, but not until the fourth quarter. One play later, cornerback Charles Woodson—Green Bay's best free agent since Reggie White—suffered a broken collarbone and wouldn't return. Earlier in that second quarter, wideout Donald Driver left with an ankle injury and he wouldn't be back, either.

With the Packers shorthanded and scrambling defensively on that final series of the first half, Pittsburgh took full advantage. Roethlisberger threw for all 77 yards of the drive—highlighted by an eight-yard TD to Ward—and the Steelers pulled to within 21–10 just 39 seconds before halftime.

During the 30-minute intermission, an emotionally distraught Woodson tried addressing his teammates. "I was pretty emotional so I didn't get a whole lot out," Woodson said. "But just to tell them to get it done." His message was heard.

"He could barely say much, he was very

emotional and choked up," safety Charlie Peprah said of Woodson. "He got about three words out. He just said, 'You know how bad I want this,' and we knew what we had to do." It certainly wasn't easy, though.

With Woodson and Shields sidelined, Green Bay was searching for defensive answers. But the Packers didn't have any early in the third quarter. After the Packers went three-and-out to start the half—a series that included a drop from James Jones that might have gone for a touchdown—Pittsburgh took over at midfield. Five running plays later, the Steelers had gone 50 yards, and Mendenhall was in the end zone.

Green Bay's lead, once as many as 18 points, had been whittled to 21–17. "It was tough," Packers defensive coordinator Dom Capers said. "We were scrambling there for a while, because a big part of our game plan went out the window. We planned on playing a lot of man coverage, and when those guys went out, we had to become more of a zone team."

Green Bay's struggles continued. One series after Jones had a critical drop, Nelson had a drop of his own—one of his three on the day—leading to a Packers punt. Green Bay's defense got a much-needed stop, but two offensive series later, Packers No. 5 wideout Brett Swain had a brutal drop. McCarthy challenged the play—and lost—and the Packers punted from deep in their territory.

"I'd say the whole game was a little bit different, not a lot of flow to it," Rodgers said. "After the pick six, we were on the sidelines for a long time in the first half. Never really got our momentum back until the fourth quarter on those last few drives. In a game like this with the long TV timeouts, you lose your sweat. You lose your feel."

The Packers had clearly lost their feel. And with the fourth quarter set to start, Pittsburgh had reached the Packers' 33-yard line trailing by just four points. On the first play of the quarter, though, Packers defensive end Ryan Pickett and linebacker Clay Matthews combined to blow up Mendenhall. Matthews stood him up on the front side, while Pickett got his helmet on the ball from behind and forced a fumble that linebacker Desmond Bishop recovered.

The Packers were back in business at Pittsburgh's 45-yard line, and Rodgers wasn't going to waste this golden opportunity.

> # "THIS TEAM THRIVES ON FORCING TURNOVERS, AND IF WE CAN HANG ON TO THE FOOTBALL AND NOT TURN IT OVER WE ARE GOING TO HAVE A GOOD CHANCE TO WIN. —Aaron Rodgers

He proceeded to make three huge throws that gave Green Bay some comfort again. The first came on a third-and-7, when Rodgers rolled right and away from trouble. Jones ran a comeback route, and Rodgers drilled him for a 12-yard gain to keep the drive alive.

Then, after Nelson dropped a crossing route for a certain first down, the Packers faced a third-and-10 from Pittsburgh's 40. The Steelers rushed five, but couldn't get close to Rodgers, in large part because running back Brandon Jackson stoned McFadden in the hole. Nelson had single coverage and whipped Clark on an inside slant. The terrific blocking up front allowed Rodgers to step into the throw, and he delivered a strike to Nelson that went for 38 yards to Pittsburgh's 2-yard line.

"If you play this game long enough in this position, you are going to drop the ball," Nelson said. "You have to move on. We are level-headed. We don't get too high and we don't get too low as a whole wide receiver core. We weren't panicking at all when Pittsburgh started coming back. We just said, okay we have to go make plays. We knew it was going to be on us, and that is why we stepped up and made plays."

Rodgers and Jennings combined to make Green Bay's next big play. After Rodgers took a sack, the Packers had second-and-goal from Pittsburgh's 8-yard line. Green Bay employed an empty backfield, and after the ball was snapped, Rodgers quickly looked left.

Rodgers had no intention of ever going left, mind you. He was simply trying to get Polamalu—the NFL's Defensive Player of the Year—to drift that way. It was a contin-

Aaron Rodgers looks for a target downfield in the second half of Super Bowl XLV.

> ## "WE WEREN'T PANICKING AT ALL WHEN PITTSBURGH STARTED COMING BACK.… WE KNEW IT WAS GOING TO BE ON US, AND THAT IS WHY WE STEPPED UP AND MADE PLAYS."
>
> —Jordy Nelson

uation of a 60-minute battle that Rodgers waged—and won—with Polamalu. "He's a guy that you have to be aware of him, where he's at all times," Rodgers said of Polamalu. "He's a great player, had a great season, but guys have to respect where my eyes are looking so it was important to me to use good eye control on the field and not stare anybody down because he can cover a lot of ground quickly.

"When he was down in the box, we made sure he was picked up in the protection schemes. A couple of times when he came on blitzes, we adjusted the protection to make sure we had him picked up because he's a very talented blitzer, and when he's high, a deep safety, you just have to make sure you are good with your eyes."

Rodgers was sublime on this play. Polamalu watched Rodgers' eyes and cheated back to the left, which allowed Jennings to come free in the right corner. Rodgers lofted another perfect ball, and Jennings' TD grab gave Green Bay a 28–17 lead. "That was completely my fault," Polamalu said afterward. "Earlier in the game they ran Jennings down the middle, and I was anticipating that same pass play and I guessed wrong."

Pittsburgh answered right back, though, as Roethlisberger engineered a 66-yard TD drive that took just seven plays and slightly more than four minutes. The Steelers' scoring strike came when Wallace got behind Shields, and Roethlisberger put the ball right on his fingertips for a 25-yard touchdown.

Antwaan Randle El scored on an option pitch for the two-point conversion, and the Steelers were within 28–25. There was still 7:34 left in what had become a Super Bowl thriller. "I thought we were going to win," Wallace said. "We never think we are going to lose. We have no doubt in our mind that we are going to win the game."

Rodgers and the Packers took over on their 25, but after a sack and a false-start penalty on Daryn Colledge, they quickly faced a third-and-10. Pittsburgh rushed just three, which meant Rodgers would have to be razor sharp to beat the eight-man coverage in back. Jennings, working from the left slot, ran another seam route against Steelers No. 1 cornerback Ike Taylor. The ball was out of Rodgers' hands in 2.8 seconds, and he had perhaps a 12-inch window to squeeze the ball into.

He did. It was arguably the throw of Rodgers' life, one that went for 31 yards and kept the Steelers' offense grounded. "It seemed like it brushed off the tip of Ike Taylor's glove," Jennings said. "But it just got over the top enough where I could

Greg Jennings and Aaron Rodgers hooked up for two touchdowns in the Super Bowl.

make a play on it." A pair of runs by James Starks netted 15 yards.

Rodgers then threw a gorgeous back shoulder pass to Jones for 21 yards to Pittsburgh's 8-yard line. On third-and-goal, though, Rodgers' fade for Nelson in the right corner of the end zone missed by inches. Green Bay was forced to settle for a Mason Crosby field goal, and its lead was a precarious 31–25 with 2:07 still remaining.

"I was just disappointed we didn't finish off with seven," Rodgers said. "We talked about it with seven minutes left when we got the ball. 'Hey, let's take it down and score, and we're the champs.' We made a couple of big plays on third down, but unfortunately, I just missed Jordy (Nelson) on that third down on the goal line. I was just praying our guys would come up with one more stop."

Two years earlier, Roethlisberger led the Steelers 78 yards in the closing moments of Super Bowl XLIII and hit Holmes with a six-yard TD pass to win the game. Then in 2009, Roethlisberger and Wallace hooked up on a 19-yard TD on the final play of the game to defeat Green Bay, 37–36. Now, Roethlisberger would get a chance to repeat history.

"We've been doing this all year long," said Tramon Williams, Green Bay's magnificent cornerback. "The defense has been put in that situation and that spot all year long, and we rose to the challenge each and every time. That's one thing we emphasized all season; that when adversity hits, that's when we want to step up and make plays, and we did that all year long."

Never more so than in the final two minutes. Pittsburgh began from its own 13 after a special teams penalty, but two Roethlisberger completions quickly took the ball to the 33. The Steelers seemed to have communication issues, though, and Roethlisberger threw consecutive incompletions to Wallace and Ward on balls that weren't even close. Now it was fourth-and-5, and Super Bowl XLV came down to one play. For the Packers, it was simple: make a stop and win a title. "Everybody was just praying," Shields said.

Green Bay rushed five and ran a fire zone in back. Roethlisberger threw to his left for Wallace, but Williams broke on the ball perfectly and knocked it to the ground. The Steelers wanted a pass interference call, but Williams' technique was perfect, and no flags were warranted. Green Bay had held. Only 49 seconds remained.

"It was a great feeling because you knew that you had to go in and keep them from scoring a touchdown in the two-minute drill," Capers said. "A year ago when we played them up there, we had the same situation, and they scored on the last play of the game to beat us. So it was a great feeling to see the play get made. That's the best feeling in the world."

There was one better: the kneel down. With Kuhn and Jackson huddled close, Rodgers took consecutive snaps and dropped to a knee. As the final seconds ticked off, Rodgers kept the ball in his hands, and that certainly seemed appropriate. Of all the reasons Green Bay had won its fourth Super Bowl and 13th NFL championship, Rodgers topped the list.

Rodgers was as crisp as a quarterback could be, and his 304 passing yards might have been 450 if it wasn't for the drops. His passer rating of 111.5 was the fourth-highest in Super Bowl history. Most importantly, though, Rodgers was terrific in taking care of the ball. He threw three TD passes, didn't have an interception or fumble, and was an easy choice for MVP.

Hoisting the championship hardware, Rodgers celebrates the Packers' NFL championship with teammate Clay Matthews.

"He made plays," Steelers coach Mike Tomlin said of Rodgers. "We didn't get turnovers. We know that they're capable of getting plays in chunks. We knew that they would throw the football quite a bit, and they did. He didn't fold under the pressure. I thought we hit him some early, we got to him as the game went on. But he showed his metal and continued to stand in there and throw the football and throw it accurately. I tip my hat to him for that."

So did Rodgers' teammates and coaches. "To be honest, I didn't expect anything less from A-Rod," Packers nose tackle B.J. Raji said. "He's been doing this the whole season throughout the playoffs. He's emerged as our leader, and I believe the best is yet to come for him."

McCarthy couldn't have agreed more. "He played great," McCarthy said. "We put everything on his shoulders. He did a lot at the line of scrimmage for us against a great defense. He did a hell of a job." Truthfully, so did the entire 2010 Packers.

Left dead when injuries struck, counted out when they were 8–6, the Packers never folded. And that resiliency, toughness, and heart led to an improbable six-game winning streak and a Super Bowl title to finish the season. "The Super Bowl was the way our whole season was in one win," Bishop said. "Ups, downs, roller coaster rides, people getting hurt, and a momentum swing; we showed resilience again. We just kept fighting and stayed as one."

Added Woodson, "We just continued to get better all season. We continued to fight no matter what adversity we went through. I think late in the season, down the stretch, we just had fun, and today was no different, and world champs." World champs is right.

The Vince Lombardi Trophy was headed back to Green Bay. Rodgers was able to don his title belt. And Green Bay's fans chanted 'Go Pack Go' while basking in the glow of another championship. "The character in that locker room is like nothing I've ever been a part of," Rodgers said. "It's just a special group of guys who believe in each other and love each other. When someone goes down, somebody steps up and picks each other up."

That had been the case again on this glorious night. Rodgers and the Packers were champions of the football world. ■

Aaron Rodgers was giddy after leading the Packers past the Steelers in Super Bowl XLV.

CHAPTER 11

SUPER GOAL:
"WIN ANOTHER ONE"

The Green Bay Packers had been NFL champions for less than an hour. Aaron Rodgers had been named the Most Valuable Player of Super Bowl XLV. He had been given the championship wrestling belt by teammate Clay Matthews. And the celebration of Green Bay's 13th championship—and fourth Super Bowl title—was in full swing. Of course, we're a forward-thinking society. So Rodgers was immediately asked if the Packers could repeat in 2011.

"I mean, we'll get Jermichael Finley back. That'll help," Rodgers said of his standout tight end. "I'm just going to enjoy tonight with my guys. It's a great feeling. It really is. It's just a feeling of accomplishment right now. We've accomplished our goals. We talked about it March 16 [2010] when we met for the first

time, and here we are, world champions. We are going to enjoy tonight, enjoy the offseason, and then try to get back here and win another one."

No team has won consecutive Super Bowl championships since New England following the 2003 and 2004 seasons. The last NFC team to win consecutive titles was Dallas following the 1992 and '93 seasons. The 2011 Packers certainly seem poised, though, to make a run at back-to-back crowns, something that hasn't happened in Green Bay since the 1966 and '67 seasons.

"Coming out of training camp it was the best football team that I stood in front of," Packers coach Mike McCarthy said of his team. "I knew that we were going to have an excellent opportunity to win the Super Bowl. When you look at

Aaron Rodgers, raising the Vince Lombardi Trophy at the "Return to Titletown" celebration, is the new golden boy of Green Bay.

"I THINK THE CORE, THE NUCLEUS OF THIS TEAM, IS INTACT TO MAKE RUNS LIKE THIS FOR THE NEXT FOUR OR FIVE YEARS. —Aaron Rodgers

our returning roster next year, it's going to be the same type of situation. I'll be very excited coaching these guys. This is a great core group. Our locker room is better than it's ever been. Winning definitely helps it, no doubt about it. I'll be very excited, just like the rest of the coaching staff, to get started when it comes around."

Green Bay became the first No. 6 seed from the NFC to ever win a Super Bowl. And the Packers joined the 2007 New York Giants as the only NFC teams to win three playoff road games on their way to the crown. What made the Packers' feat even more impressive was that they did it despite being hammered with injury.

Six opening-day starters wound up on the injured reserve list and missed a combined total of 97 games (including playoffs). The Packers finished the regular season with 15 players on injured reserve,

including eight that started a game. In addition, five other "preferred" starters missed time in 2010. With standouts like Finley, running back Ryan Grant, safety Morgan Burnett, defensive end Mike Neal, and linebacker Nick Barnett all expected back, the Packers should have the NFL's most talented roster.

"It's a challenge, but I feel like we are kind of reloading," Rodgers said. "We are going to have the best tight end in the NFL back into the mix here. I think we are getting, I think 15 guys back from I.R. I'm sure a number of those guys will be back.

"It will be a different team. Every team has a different face to it, every year, different players, guys come and go, but I think the core, the nucleus of this team, is intact to make runs like this for the next four or five years." Of course talent alone doesn't win championships. Many would

With a Super Bowl title and MVP on his résumé, Aaron Rodgers could become one of the NFL's most marketable players.

Game-winning pass.
Ever since I was a kid, my mom
and coach taught me that to play my best,
I need to fuel up to play 60. And one of
the best ways to do that is with milk. Even
now that I'm a Super Bowl champion,
milk's still part of my game plan.
Make it part of yours.

got milk?

whymilk.com/aaronrodgers

argue that the 2010 Packers weren't the most talented outfit in football, but they had terrific chemistry, clicked at the right time, and played their best football when it mattered most.

"Talent. That's such a dynamic word and component of your football team," McCarthy said. "I think it's a great lesson for everyone in our building to learn. The most important thing is we need to be the best football team again next year. We can be maybe the most talented and best football team. But sometimes the most talented team doesn't win. We were the best football team in the National Football League this year and lost a lot of talent due to injuries. It's a great experience for us to learn from. It will be a great experience for us to draw from.

"Yes, we have an opportunity to start the season as a very talented football team. But we have to make sure we're the best football team, that everybody's doing their role, doing what they're supposed to be doing at the level they're supposed to be doing it. Because that was a great experience to watch this group of men pull together and fight through the adversity that they needed to and play their best football when it counted."

Of course, no one played better than Rodgers, who has spent his life trying to prove people wrong. First, it was the Division I colleges that didn't recruit him. Next, it was the NFL general managers that made him wait on draft day. Finally, it was the Brett Favre fans that insisted the Packers made a mistake going with Rodgers back in 2008, after he'd waited three years for a shot.

So now what? "I'm always looking for challenges," Rodgers said. "I think the challenge now goes to repeating, scrutinizing this season, finding ways to get better. There's going to be plenty of time to work on things and plenty of things to work on."

That could be a scary thought for the rest of the NFL, because it seems like Rodgers and these Packers are just getting warmed up. ■

Aaron Rodgers capped his remarkable Super Bowl week by winning Most Valuable Player honors.